SAMSUNG

USER MANUAL

SM-G960F
SM-G960F/DS
SM-G965F
SM-G965F/DS

English. 12/2018. Rev.1.0

www.samsung.com

Table of Contents

Basics

- 4 Read me first
- 7 Device overheating situations and solutions
- 11 Device layout and functions
- 18 Battery
- 23 SIM or USIM card (nano-SIM card)
- 29 Memory card (microSD card)
- 33 Turning the device on and off
- 34 Initial setup
- 36 Samsung account
- 38 Transferring data from your previous device (Smart Switch)
- 42 Understanding the screen
- 56 Notification panel
- 58 Entering text

Apps and features

- 61 Installing or uninstalling apps
- 63 Bixby
- 72 Bixby Vision
- 76 Bixby Home
- 78 Reminder
- 82 Phone
- 87 Contacts
- 91 Messages
- 95 Internet
- 97 Email
- 98 Camera
- 129 Gallery
- 136 Always On Display
- 139 Edge screen
- 143 Multi window
- 146 Kids Home
- 148 Samsung Pay
- 151 Galaxy Wearable
- 152 Samsung Members
- 153 Samsung Notes
- 154 Calendar
- 155 Samsung Health
- 161 Voice Recorder
- 163 My Files
- 163 Clock
- 165 Calculator
- 166 Game Launcher
- 169 SmartThings
- 174 Sharing content
- 175 Samsung DeX
- 181 Google apps

Table of Contents

Settings

183 Introduction
183 Connections
    184 Wi-Fi
    187 Bluetooth
    189 NFC and payment
    192 Data saver
    193 SIM card manager (dual SIM models)
    193 Mobile Hotspot and Tethering
    195 More connection settings
198 Sounds and vibration
    198 Dolby Atmos (surround sound)
    199 Separate app sound
199 Notifications
    200 App icon badges
200 Display
    202 Blue light filter
    202 Changing the screen mode or adjusting the display colour
    204 Screen resolution
    204 Screensaver
205 Wallpapers and themes
205 Lock screen
    206 Smart Lock
207 Biometrics and security
    209 Intelligent Scan
    212 Face recognition
    215 Iris recognition
    220 Fingerprint recognition
    223 Samsung Pass
    228 Secure Folder
233 Accounts and backup
    234 Samsung Cloud

235 Google
236 Advanced features
    237 Dual Messenger
238 Device care
240 Apps
241 General management
242 Accessibility
242 Software update
243 User manual
243 About phone

Appendix

244 Accessibility
261 Troubleshooting
268 Removing the battery

3

Basics

Read me first

Please read this manual before using the device to ensure safe and proper use.

- Descriptions are based on the device's default settings.
- Some content may differ from your device depending on the region, service provider, model specifications, or device's software.
- Content (high quality content) that requires high CPU and RAM usage will affect the overall performance of the device. Apps related to the content may not work properly depending on the device's specifications and the environment that it is used in.
- Samsung is not liable for performance issues caused by apps supplied by providers other than Samsung.
- Samsung is not liable for performance issues or incompatibilities caused by edited registry settings or modified operating system software. Attempting to customise the operating system may cause the device or apps to work improperly.
- Software, sound sources, wallpapers, images, and other media provided with this device are licensed for limited use. Extracting and using these materials for commercial or other purposes is an infringement of copyright laws. Users are entirely responsible for illegal use of media.
- You may incur additional charges for data services, such as messaging, uploading and downloading, auto-syncing, or using location services depending on your data plan. For large data transfers, it is recommended to use the Wi-Fi feature.
- Default apps that come with the device are subject to updates and may no longer be supported without prior notice. If you have questions about an app provided with the device, contact a Samsung Service Centre. For user-installed apps, contact service providers.

Basics

- Modifying the device's operating system or installing softwares from unofficial sources may result in device malfunctions and data corruption or loss. These actions are violations of your Samsung licence agreement and will void your warranty.
- Depending on the region or service provider, a screen protector is attached for protection during production and distribution. Damage to the attached screen protector is not covered by the warranty.
- You can see the touchscreen clearly even in strong outdoor sunlight by automatically adjusting the contrast range based on the surrounding environment. Due to the nature of the product, displaying fixed graphics for extended periods may result in afterimages (screen burn-in) or ghosting.
    – It is recommended not to use fixed graphics on part or all of the touchscreen for extended periods and turn off the touchscreen when not using the device.
    – You can set the touchscreen to turn off automatically when you are not using it. Launch the **Settings** app, tap **Display** → **Screen timeout**, and then select the length of time you want the device to wait before turning off the touchscreen.
    – To set the touchscreen to automatically adjust its brightness based on the surrounding environment, launch the **Settings** app, tap **Display**, and then tap the **Adaptive brightness** switch to activate it.
- Depending on the region or model, some devices are required to receive approval from the Federal Communications Commission (FCC). If your device is approved by the FCC, you can view the FCC ID of the device. To view the FCC ID, launch the **Settings** app and tap **About phone** → **Status**.
- Depending on the region, you can view the regulatory information on the device. To view the information, launch the **Settings** app and tap **About phone** → **Regulatory information**.

5

Basics

Maintaining water and dust resistance

Your device supports water- and dust-resistance. Follow these tips carefully to maintain the water- and dust-resistance of your device. Failure to do so may result in damage to your device.

- Do not immerse the device in fresh water deeper than 1.5 m or keep it submerged for more than 30 minutes. If you immerse the device in any liquid other than fresh water, such as salt water, ionised water, or alcoholic beverage, liquid will enter the device faster.
- Do not expose the device to **water moving with force**.
- If the device is exposed to fresh water, dry it thoroughly with a clean, soft cloth. If the device is exposed to other liquids, such as salt water, swimming pool water, soapy water, oil, perfume, sunscreen, hand cleaner, or chemical products such as cosmetics, rinse it with fresh water and dry it thoroughly with a clean, soft cloth. If you do not follow these instructions, the device's performance and appearance may be affected.
- **If the device has been immersed in water or the microphone or speaker is wet**, sound may not be heard clearly during a call. After wiping the device with a dry cloth, dry it thoroughly before using it.
- The touchscreen and other features may not work properly **if the device is used in water**.
- **If the device is dropped or receives an impact**, the water- and dust-resistant features of the device may be damaged.
- Your device has been tested in a controlled environment and certified to be water- and dust-resistant in specific situations (meets requirements of classification IP68 as described by the international standard IEC 60529-Degrees of Protection provided by Enclosures [IP Code]; test conditions: 15-35 °C, 86-106 kPa, fresh water, 1.5 metre, 30 minutes). Despite this classification, it is still possible for your device to be damaged in certain situations.

Instructional icons

 Warning: situations that could cause injury to yourself or others

 Caution: situations that could cause damage to your device or other equipment

 Notice: notes, usage tips, or additional information

Basics

Device overheating situations and solutions

When the device heats up while charging the battery

While charging, the device and the charger may become hot. During wireless charging or fast charging, the device may feel hotter to the touch. This does not affect the device's lifespan or performance and is in the device's normal range of operation. If the battery becomes too hot, the charger may stop charging.

Do the following when the device heats up:

- Disconnect the charger from the device and close any running apps. Wait for the device to cool down and then begin charging the device again.
- If the lower part of the device overheats, it could be because the connected USB cable is damaged. Replace the damaged USB cable with a new Samsung-approved one.
- When using a wireless charger, do not place foreign materials, such as metal objects, magnets, and magnetic stripe cards, between the device and the wireless charger.

  The wireless charging or fast charging feature is only available on supported models.

7

Basics

When the device heats up during use

When you use features or apps that require more power or use them for extended periods, your device may temporarily heat up due to increased battery consumption. Close any running apps and do not use the device for a while.

The following are examples of situations in which the device may overheat. Depending on the functions and apps you use, these examples may not apply to your model.

- During the initial setup after purchase or when restoring data
- When downloading large files
- When using apps that require more power or using apps for extended periods
    - When playing high-quality games for extended periods
    - When recording videos for extended periods
    - When streaming videos while using the maximum brightness setting
    - When connecting to a TV
- While multitasking (or, when running many apps in the background)
    - When using Multi window
    - When updating or installing apps while recording videos
    - When downloading large files during a video call
    - When recording videos while using a navigation app
- When using large amount of data for syncing with the cloud, email, or other accounts
- When using a navigation app in a car while the device is placed in direct sunlight
- When using the mobile hotspot and tethering feature
- When using the device in areas with weak signals or no reception
- When charging the battery with a damaged USB cable
- When the device's multipurpose jack is damaged or exposed to foreign materials, such as liquid, dust, metal powder, and pencil lead
- When you are roaming

Basics

Do the following when the device heats up:

- Keep the device updated with the latest software.
- Conflicts between running apps may cause the device to heat up. Restart the device.
- Deactivate the Wi-Fi, GPS, and Bluetooth features when not using them.
- Close apps that increase battery consumption or that run in the background when not in use.
- Delete unnecessary files or unused apps.
- Decrease the screen brightness.
- If the device overheats or feels hot for a prolonged period, do not use it for a while. If the device continues to overheat, contact a Samsung Service Centre.

Device limitations when the device overheats

When the device heats up, the features and performance may be limited or the device may turn off to cool down. The feature is only available on supported models.

- If the device becomes hotter than usual, a device overheating message will appear. To lower the device's temperature, the screen brightness and the performance speed will be limited and battery charging will stop. Running apps will be closed and you will only be able to make emergency calls until the device cools down.
- If the device overheats or feels hot for a prolonged period, a power off message will appear. Turn off the device, and wait until it cools down.

Precautions for operating environment

Your device may heat up due to the environment in the following conditions. Use caution to avoid shortening the battery's lifespan, damaging the device, or causing a fire.

- Do not store your device in very cold or very hot temperatures.
- Do not expose your device to direct sunlight for extended periods.
- Do not use or store your device for extended periods in very hot areas, such as inside a car in the summertime.
- Do not place the device in any areas that may overheat, such as on an electric heating mat.
- Do not store your device near or in heaters, microwaves, hot cooking equipment, or high pressure containers.
- Never use a damaged charger or battery.

Basics

Device layout and functions

Package contents

Refer to the quick start guide for package contents.

- The items supplied with the device and any available accessories may vary depending on the region or service provider.
- The supplied items are designed only for this device and may not be compatible with other devices.
- Appearances and specifications are subject to change without prior notice.
- You can purchase additional accessories from your local Samsung retailer. Make sure they are compatible with the device before purchase.
- Use only Samsung-approved accessories. Using unapproved accessories may cause the performance problems and malfunctions that are not covered by the warranty.
- Availability of all accessories is subject to change depending entirely on manufacturing companies. For more information about available accessories, refer to the Samsung website.

Basics

Device layout

▶ **Galaxy S9 models:**

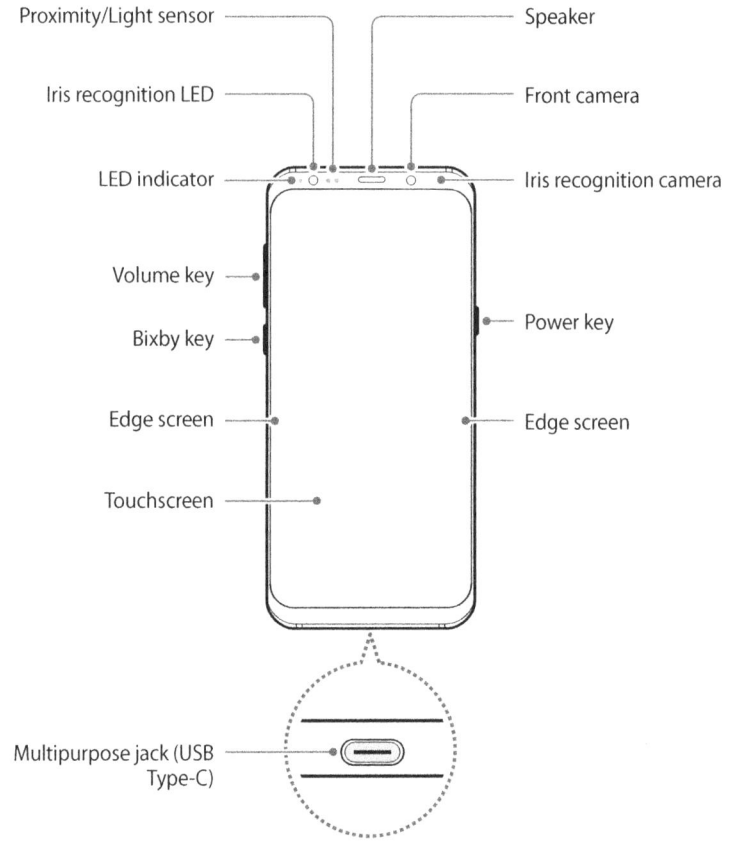

Basics

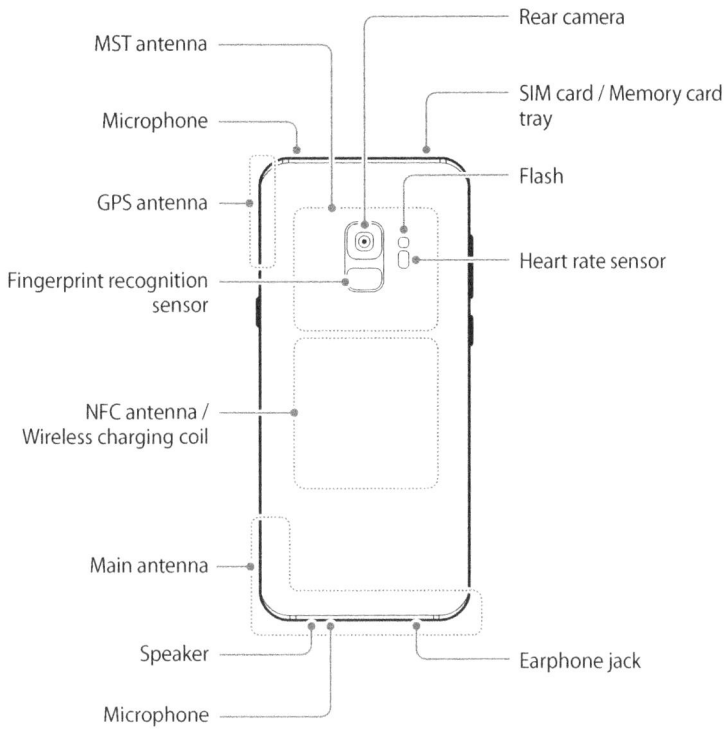

Basics

▶ **Galaxy S9+ models:**

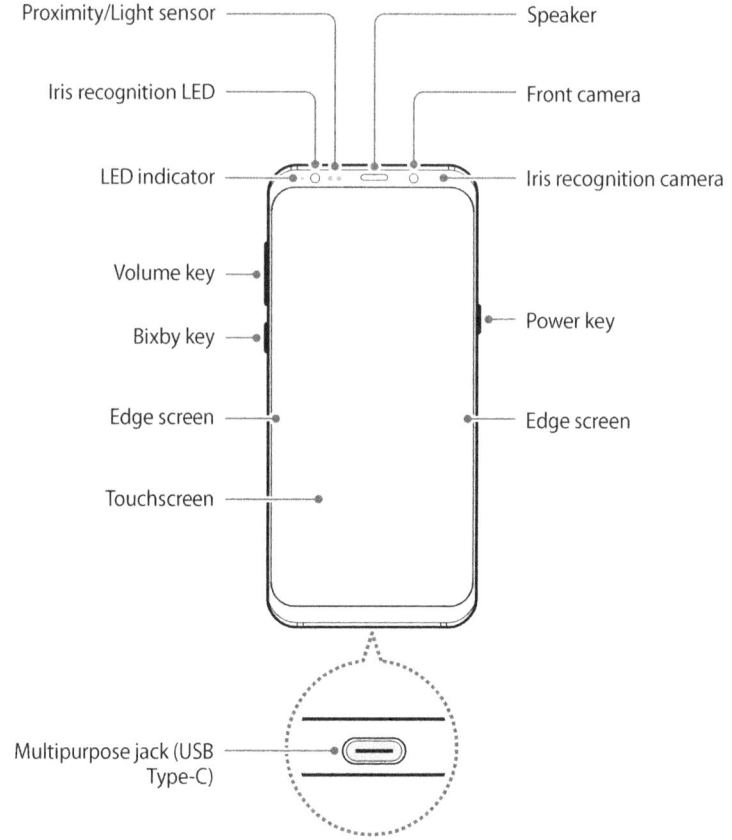

Basics

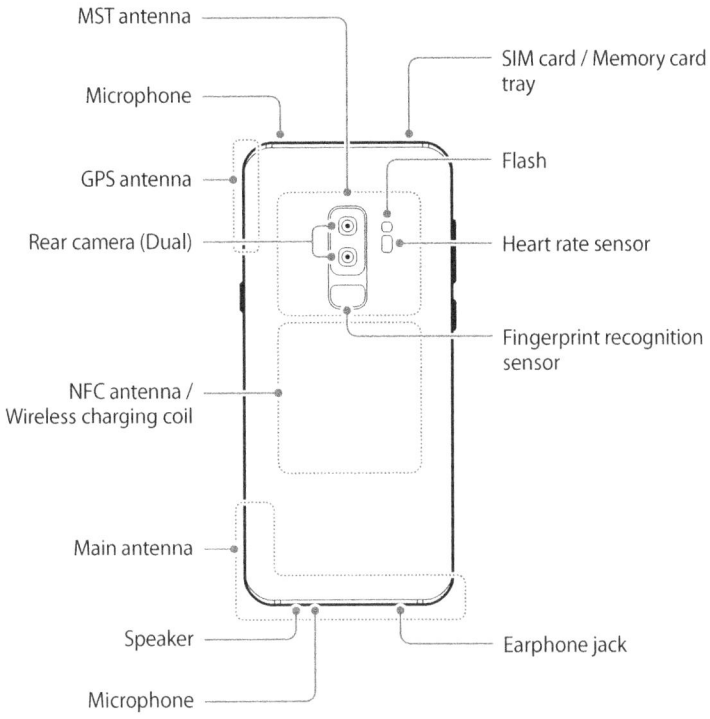

- When using the speakers, such as when playing media files or using speakerphone, do not place the device close to your ears.
- Be careful not to expose the camera lens to a strong light source, such as direct sunlight. If the camera lens is exposed to a strong light source, such as direct sunlight, the camera image sensor may be damaged. A damaged image sensor is irreparable and will cause dots or spots in pictures.

Basics

 • Connectivity problems and battery drain may occur in the following situations:
  – If you attach metallic stickers on the antenna area of the device
  – If you attach a device cover made with metallic material to the device
  – If you cover the device's antenna area with your hands or other objects while using certain features, such as calls or the mobile data connection
• Using a Samsung-approved screen protector is recommended. Unapproved screen protectors may cause the sensors to malfunction.
• Do not cover the proximity/light sensor area with screen accessories, such as a screen protector or stickers. Doing so may cause the sensor to malfunction.
• The colours on the Edge screen may look different depending on your viewing position.

Hard keys

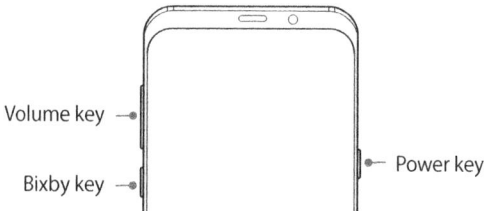

Volume key
Bixby key
Power key

Key	Function
Power	• Press and hold to turn the device on or off. • Press to turn on or lock the screen.
Bixby	• Press to launch Bixby. Refer to Bixby for more information. • Press and hold to start a conversation with Bixby. Refer to Using Bixby for more information.
Volume	• Press to adjust the device volume.

Basics

Soft buttons

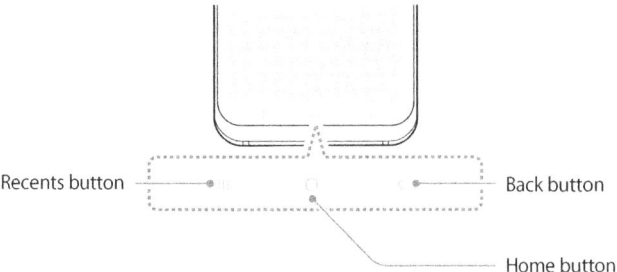

Recents button — Back button — Home button

When you turn on the screen, the soft buttons will appear at the bottom of the screen. The soft buttons are set to the Recents button, Home button, and Back button by default. Refer to Navigation bar (soft buttons) for more information.

Basics

Battery

Charging the battery

Charge the battery before using it for the first time or when it has been unused for extended periods.

 Use only Samsung-approved chargers, batteries, and cables. Unapproved chargers or cables can cause the battery to explode or damage the device.

- Connecting the charger improperly may cause serious damage to the device. Any damage caused by misuse is not covered by the warranty.
- Use only USB Type-C cable supplied with the device. The device may be damaged if you use Micro USB cable.

 To save energy, unplug the charger when not in use. The charger does not have a power switch, so you must unplug the charger from the electric socket when not in use to avoid wasting power. The charger should remain close to the electric socket and easily accessible while charging.

1 Connect the USB cable to the USB power adaptor.

2 Plug the USB cable into the device's multipurpose jack.

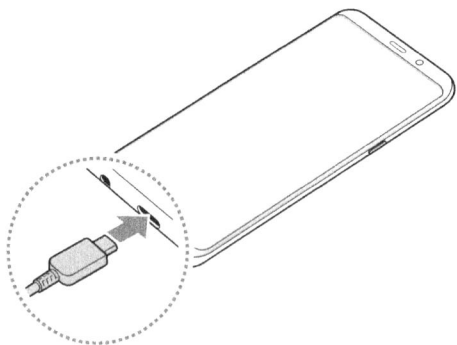

18

Basics

3 Plug the USB power adaptor into an electric socket.

4 After fully charging, disconnect the charger from the device. Then, unplug the charger from the electric socket.

Charging other devices

Use the USB connector (USB Type-C) to charge another mobile device with your device's battery.

Plug the USB connector (USB Type-C) into your device's multipurpose jack, and connect your device and the other device via the other device's USB cable.

When charging starts, the battery charging icon will appear on the other device's screen.

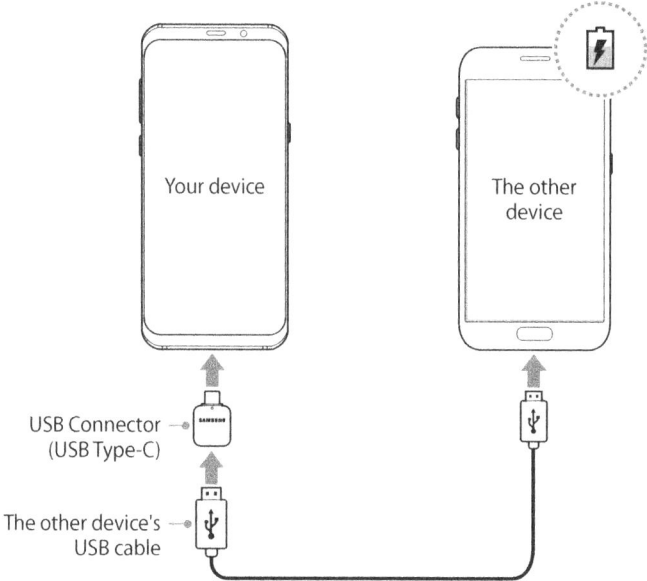

 The app selection pop-up window that appears on your device is for data transfer. Do not select an app from the pop-up window.

Basics

Reducing the battery consumption

Your device provides various options that help you conserve battery power.
- Optimise the device using the device care feature.
- When you are not using the device, turn off the screen by pressing the Power key.
- Activate power saving mode.
- Close unnecessary apps.
- Deactivate the Bluetooth feature when not in use.
- Deactivate the Wi-Fi feature when not in use.
- Deactivate auto-syncing of apps that need to be synced.
- Decrease the backlight time.
- Decrease the screen brightness.

Battery charging tips and precautions

- When the battery power is low, the battery icon appears empty.
- If the battery is completely discharged, the device cannot be turned on immediately when the charger is connected. Allow a depleted battery to charge for a few minutes before turning on the device.
- If you use multiple apps at once, network apps, or apps that need a connection to another device, the battery will drain quickly. To avoid losing power during a data transfer, always use these apps after fully charging the battery.
- Using a power source other than the charger, such as a computer, may result in a slower charging speed due to a lower electric current.
- The device can be used while it is charging, but it may take longer to fully charge the battery.
- If the device receives an unstable power supply while charging, the touchscreen may not function. If this happens, unplug the charger from the device.

Basics

- While charging, the device and the charger may heat up. This is normal and should not affect the device's lifespan or performance. If the battery gets hotter than usual, the charger may stop charging.
- If you charge the device while the multipurpose jack is wet, the device may be damaged. Thoroughly dry the multipurpose jack before charging the device.
- If the device is not charging properly, take the device and the charger to a Samsung Service Centre.

Fast charging

The device has a built-in fast charging feature. You can charge the battery more quickly while the device or its screen is turned off.

Increasing the charging speed

To increase the charging speed, turn the device or its screen off when you charge the battery. While charging the battery when the device is turned off, the ⚡ icon appears on the screen.

If the fast charging feature is not activated, launch the **Settings** app, tap **Device care** → **Battery** → ⋮ → **Settings**, and then tap the **Fast cable charging** switch to activate it.

- You cannot use the built-in fast charging feature when you charge the battery using a standard battery charger.
- If the device heats up or the ambient air temperature rises, the charging speed may decrease automatically. This is a normal operating condition to prevent damage to the device.

Basics

Wireless charging

The device has a built-in wireless charging coil. You can charge the battery using a wireless charger (sold separately).

Fast wireless charging

You can charge your device faster using the fast wireless charging feature. To use this feature, you must use a charger and components that support the fast wireless charging feature.

If the fast wireless charging feature is not activated, launch the **Settings** app, tap **Device care** → **Battery** → → **Settings**, and then tap the **Fast wireless charging** switch to activate it.

- The on/off option will be added in your device's settings menu when you first place it on the charger.
- A fan inside the charger may produce noise during fast wireless charging.

Charging the battery

1 Place the centre of the device's back on the centre of the wireless charger.

The estimated charging time will appear on the screen. The actual charging time may vary depending on the charging conditions.

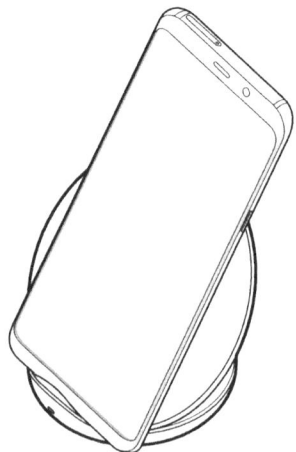

Basics

2 After fully charging, disconnect the device from the wireless charger.

Precautions for wireless charging
- Do not place the device on the wireless charger with a credit card or radio-frequency identification (RFID) card (such as a transportation card or a key card) placed between the back of the device and the device cover.
- Do not place the device on the wireless charger when conductive materials, such as metal objects and magnets, are placed between the device and the wireless charger.

The device may not charge properly or may overheat, or the device and the cards may be damaged.

- If you use the wireless charger in areas with weak network signals, you may lose network reception.
- Use Samsung-approved wireless chargers. If you use other wireless chargers, the battery may not charge properly.

SIM or USIM card (nano-SIM card)

Installing the SIM or USIM card

Insert the SIM or USIM card provided by the mobile telephone service provider.

For dual SIM models, you can insert two SIM or USIM cards so you can have two phone numbers or service providers for a single device. In some areas, data transfer speeds may be slower if two SIM cards are inserted in the device than when one SIM card is inserted.

Use caution not to lose or let others use the SIM or USIM card. Samsung is not responsible for any damages or inconveniences caused by lost or stolen cards.

Some LTE services may not be available depending on the service provider. For more information about service availability, contact your service provider.

23

Basics

► Single SIM models:

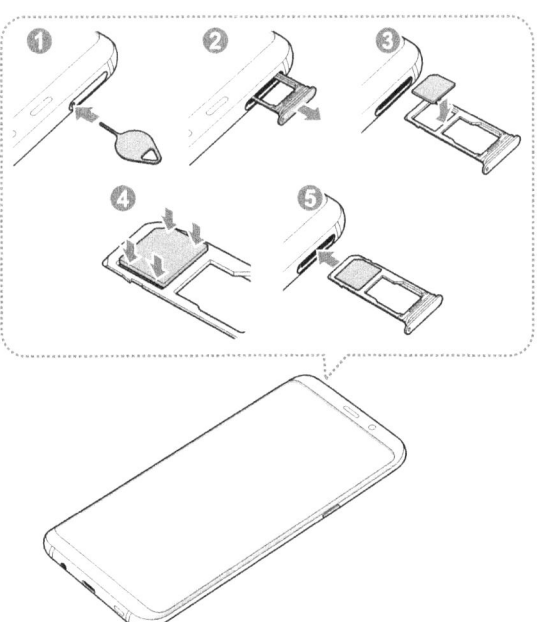

Basics

▶ Dual SIM models:

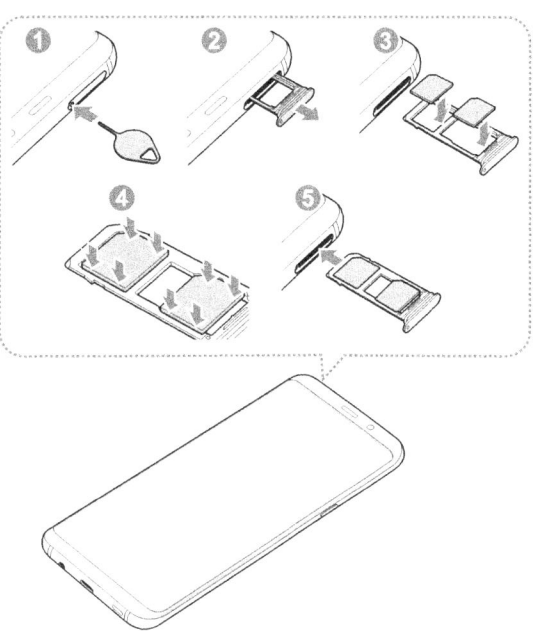

Basics

1 Insert the ejection pin into the hole on the tray to loosen the tray.

Ensure that the ejection pin is perpendicular to the hole. Otherwise, the device may be damaged.

2 Pull out the tray gently from the tray slot.

3 ▶ **Single SIM models**: Place the SIM or USIM card on the tray 1 with the gold-coloured contacts facing downwards.

▶ **Dual SIM models**: Place the SIM or USIM card on the tray with the gold-coloured contacts facing downwards. Place the primary SIM or USIM card on the tray 1 (❶) and the secondary SIM or USIM card on the tray 2 (❷).

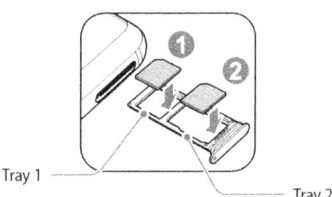

Tray 1 — Tray 2

4 Gently press the SIM or USIM card into the tray to secure it.

If the card is not fixed firmly into the tray, the SIM card may leave or fall out of the tray.

5 Insert the tray back into the tray slot.

- If you insert the tray into your device while the tray is wet, your device may be damaged. Always make sure the tray is dry.
- Fully insert the tray into the tray slot to prevent liquid from entering your device.

Correct card installation

▶ **Single SIM models:**

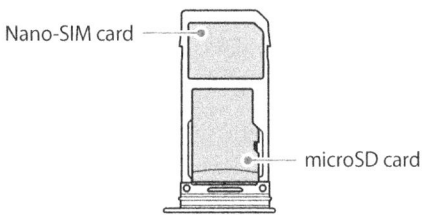

▶ **Dual SIM models:**

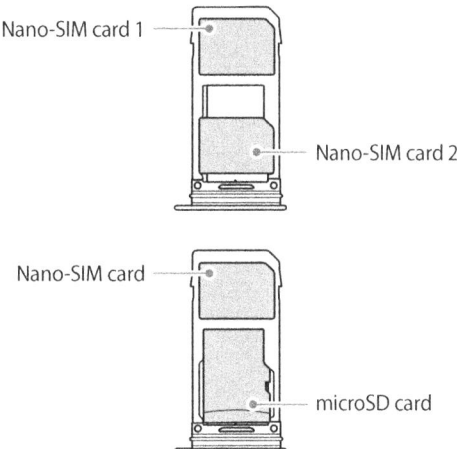

- Use only a nano-SIM card.
- You cannot insert a nano-SIM card and a microSD card in tray 2 at the same time.

Basics

Removing the SIM or USIM card

1 Insert the ejection pin into the hole on the tray to loosen the tray.

2 Pull out the tray gently from the tray slot.

3 Remove the SIM or USIM card.

4 Insert the tray back into the tray slot.

Using dual SIM or USIM cards (dual SIM models)

If you insert two SIM or USIM cards, you can have two phone numbers or service providers for a single device.

Activating SIM or USIM cards

Launch the **Settings** app and tap **Connections** → **SIM card manager**. Select a SIM or USIM card and tap the switch to activate it.

Customising SIM or USIM cards

Launch the **Settings** app, tap **Connections** → **SIM card manager**, and then select a SIM or USIM card to access the following options:

- **Icon**: Change the icon of the SIM or USIM card.
- **Name**: Change the display name of the SIM or USIM card.
- **Network mode**: Select a network type to use with the SIM or USIM card.

Setting preferred SIM or USIM cards

When two cards are activated, you can assign voice calls, messaging, and data services to specific cards.

Launch the **Settings** app, tap **Connections** → **SIM card manager**, and then set the feature preferences for your cards in **Preferred SIM card**.

Basics

Memory card (microSD card)

Installing a memory card

Your device's memory card capacity may vary from other models and some memory cards may not be compatible with your device depending on the memory card manufacturer and type. To view your device's maximum memory card capacity, refer to the Samsung website.

- Some memory cards may not be fully compatible with the device. Using an incompatible card may damage the device or the memory card, or corrupt the data stored in it.
- Use caution to insert the memory card right-side up.

- The device supports the FAT and the exFAT file systems for memory cards. When inserting a card formatted in a different file system, the device will ask to reformat the card or will not recognise the card. To use the memory card, you must format it. If your device cannot format or recognise the memory card, contact the memory card manufacturer or a Samsung Service Centre.
- Frequent writing and erasing of data shortens the lifespan of memory cards.
- When inserting a memory card into the device, the memory card's file directory appears in the **My Files** → **SD card** folder.

Basics

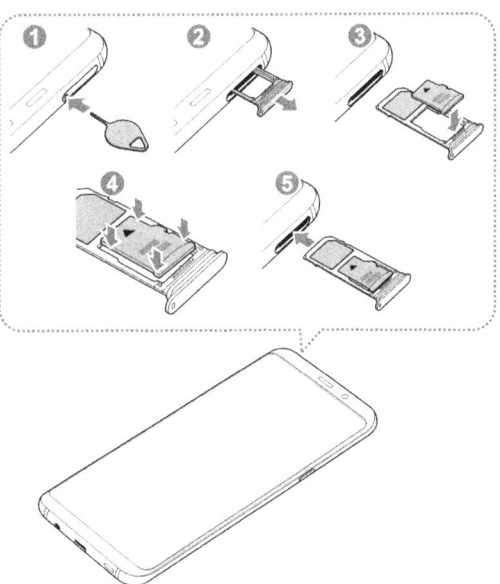

1 Insert the ejection pin into the hole on the tray to loosen the tray.

> Ensure that the ejection pin is perpendicular to the hole. Otherwise, the device may be damaged.

2 Pull out the tray gently from the tray slot.

> When you remove the tray from the device, the mobile data connection will be disabled.

Basics

3 Place a memory card on the tray 2 with the gold-coloured contacts facing downwards.

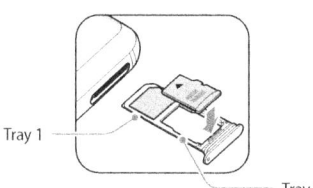

Tray 1

Tray 2

4 Gently press the memory card into the tray to secure it.

 If the card is not fixed firmly into the tray, the memory card may leave or fall out of the tray.

5 Insert the tray back into the tray slot.

- If you insert the tray into your device while the tray is wet, your device may be damaged. Always make sure the tray is dry.
- Fully insert the tray into the tray slot to prevent liquid from entering your device.

Removing the memory card

Before removing the memory card, first unmount it for safe removal.

Launch the **Settings** app and tap **Device care** → **Storage** → ⋮ → **Storage settings** → **SD card** → **Unmount**.

1 Insert the ejection pin into the hole on the tray to loosen the tray.

2 Pull out the tray gently from the tray slot.

Basics

3 Remove the memory card.

4 Insert the tray back into the tray slot.

Do not remove external storage, such as a memory card or USB storage, while the device is transferring or accessing information, or right after transferring data. Doing so can cause data to be corrupted or lost or cause damage to the external storage or device. Samsung is not responsible for losses, including loss of data, resulting from the misuse of external storage devices.

Formatting the memory card

A memory card formatted on a computer may not be compatible with the device. Format the memory card on the device.

Launch the **Settings** app and tap **Device care** → **Storage** → ⋮ → **Storage settings** → **SD card** → **Format**.

Before formatting the memory card, remember to make backup copies of all important data stored in the memory card. The manufacturer's warranty does not cover loss of data resulting from user actions.

Basics

Turning the device on and off

Press and hold the Power key for a few seconds to turn on the device.

When you turn on your device for the first time or after performing a data reset, follow the on-screen instructions to set up your device.

To turn off the device, press and hold the Power key, and then tap **Power off**.

 Follow all posted warnings and directions from authorised personnel in areas where the use of wireless devices is restricted, such as aeroplanes and hospitals.

Restarting the device

To restart the device, press and hold the Power key, and then tap **Restart**.

If your device is frozen and unresponsive, press and hold the Power key and the Volume Down key simultaneously for more than 7 seconds to restart it.

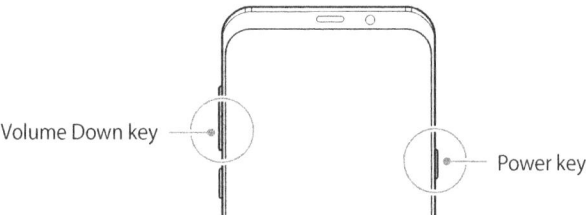

Volume Down key

Power key

Basics

Emergency mode

You can switch the device to emergency mode to reduce battery consumption. Some apps and functions will be restricted. In emergency mode, you can make an emergency call, send your current location information to others, sound an emergency alarm, and more.

Activating emergency mode

To activate emergency mode, press and hold the Power key, and then tap **Emergency mode**.

The usage time left shows the time remaining before the battery power runs out. Usage time left may vary depending on your device settings and operating conditions.

Deactivating emergency mode

To deactivate emergency mode, tap → **Turn off Emergency mode**. Alternatively, press and hold the Power key, and then tap **Emergency mode**.

Initial setup

When you turn on your device for the first time or after performing a data reset, follow the on-screen instructions to set up your device.

- The initial setup procedures may vary depending on the device's software and your region.
- You can set up your device with Bixby depending on the selected device language.

1 Turn on the device.

Basics

2 Select your preferred device language and select .

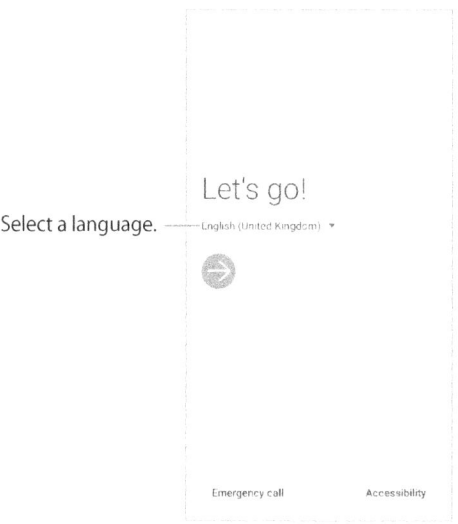

3 Read and agree to the terms and conditions and tap **Next**.

4 Get your content from a previous device.

5 Select a Wi-Fi network and connect to it.

 If you do not connect to a Wi-Fi network, you may not be able to set up some device features during the initial setup.

6 Follow the on-screen instructions to proceed the initial setup.

7 Set a screen lock method to protect your device. You can protect your personal information by preventing others from accessing your device. To set the screen lock method later, tap **Not now**.

8 If the recommended apps screen appears, select apps you want and download them.

9 Sign in to your Samsung account. You can enjoy Samsung services and keep your data up to date and secure across all of your devices. Refer to Samsung account for more information.

Basics

Samsung account

Introduction

Your Samsung account is an integrated account service that allows you to use a variety of Samsung services provided by mobile devices, TVs, and the Samsung website. Once your Samsung account has been registered, you can keep your data up to date and secure across your Samsung devices with Samsung Cloud, track and control your lost or stolen device, see tips and tricks from Samsung Members, and more.

Create your Samsung account with your email address.

To check the list of services that can be used with your Samsung account, visit account.samsung.com. For more information on Samsung accounts, launch the **Settings** app and tap **Accounts and backup** → **Accounts** → **Samsung account** → → **Help**.

Registering your Samsung account

Registering a new Samsung account

If you do not have a Samsung account, you should create one.

1. Launch the **Settings** app and tap **Accounts and backup** → **Accounts** → **Add account** → **Samsung account**.

   Alternatively, launch the **Settings** app and tap .

2. Tap **Create account**.

3. Follow the on-screen instructions to complete creating your account.

Basics

Registering an existing Samsung account

If you already have a Samsung account, register it to the device.

1 Launch the **Settings** app and tap **Accounts and backup** → **Accounts** → **Add account** → **Samsung account**.

   Alternatively, launch the **Settings** app and tap .

2 Enter your Samsung account ID and password and tap **Sign in**.

   If you forget your account information, tap **Find ID** or **Reset password**. You can find your account information when you enter the required information.

   If a pop-up window about using biometric data appears, tap **Register**. You can verify your Samsung account password via your biometric data, such as fingerprints or irises. Refer to Samsung Pass for more information.

3 Read and agree to the terms and conditions and tap **Next** to finish registering your Samsung account.

Removing your Samsung account

When you remove your registered Samsung account from the device, your data, such as contacts or events, will also be removed.

1 Launch the **Settings** app and tap **Accounts and backup** → **Accounts**.

2 Tap **Samsung account** → → **Remove account**.

3 Tap **Remove**, enter your Samsung account password, and then tap **OK**.

Basics

Transferring data from your previous device (Smart Switch)

Connect with your previous device via Smart Switch to transfer data.

Launch the **Settings** app and tap **Accounts and backup** → **Smart Switch**.

- This feature may not be supported on some devices or computers.
- Limitations apply. Visit www.samsung.com/smartswitch for details. Samsung takes copyright seriously. Only transfer content that you own or have the right to transfer.

Transferring data using a USB connector (USB Type-C)

You can connect your previous device to your device with the USB connector (USB Type-C) and a USB cable to easily and quickly transfer data.

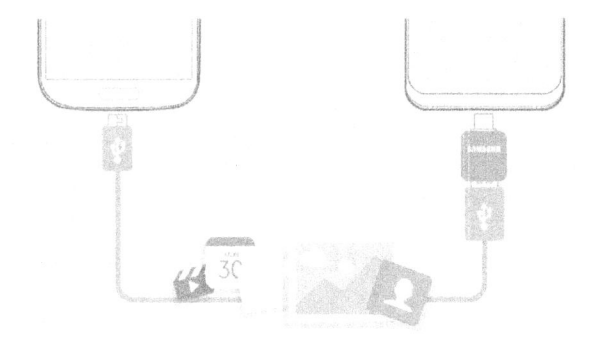

Basics

1 Plug the USB connector (USB Type-C) into the multipurpose jack of your device.

2 Connect your device and the previous device using the previous device's USB cable.

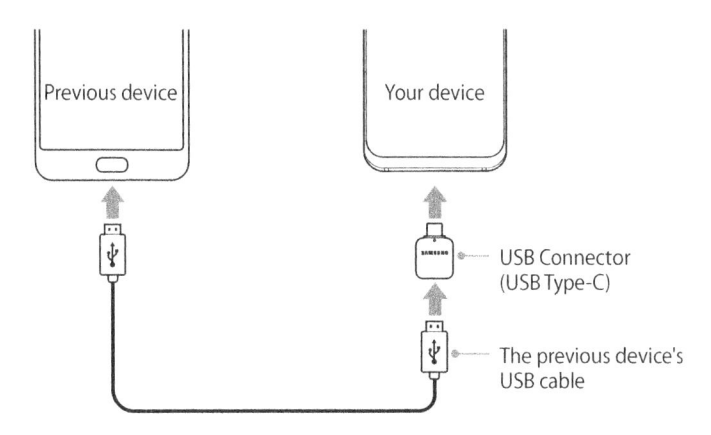

3 When the app selection pop-up window appears, tap **Smart Switch** → **Receive data**.

4 In the previous device, tap **Allow**.

   If you do not have the app, download it from **Galaxy Apps** or **Play Store**.

   Your device will recognise the previous device and a list of data you can transfer will appear.

5 Select an item to bring and tap **TRANSFER**.

6 Follow the on-screen instructions to transfer data from the previous device.

Do not disconnect the USB cable or USB connector (USB Type-C) from the device when you are transferring files. Doing so may cause data loss or device damage.

Transferring data increases the battery power consumption of your device. Ensure that your device is sufficiently charged before transferring data. If the battery power is low, data transfer may be interrupted.

Basics

Transferring data wirelessly via Wi-Fi Direct

Transfer data from your previous device to your device wirelessly via Wi-Fi Direct.

1 On the previous device, launch Smart Switch.

 If you do not have the app, download it from **Galaxy Apps** or **Play Store**.

2 On your device, launch the **Settings** app and tap **Accounts and backup** → **Smart Switch**.

3 Place the devices near each other.

4 On the previous device, tap **Send data** → **Wireless**.

5 On the previous device, select an item to transfer and tap **SEND**.

6 On your device, tap **RECEIVE**.

7 Follow the on-screen instructions to transfer data from your previous device.

Transferring data using external storage

Transfer data using external storage, such as a microSD card.

1 Transfer data from your previous device to external storage.

2 Insert or connect the external storage device to your device.

3 On your device, launch the **Settings** app and tap **Accounts and backup** → **Smart Switch** → → **Restore**.

4 Follow the on-screen instructions to transfer data from external storage.

Basics

Transferring backup data from a computer

Transfer data between your device and a computer. You must download the Smart Switch computer version app from www.samsung.com/smartswitch. Back up data from your previous device to a computer and import the data to your device.

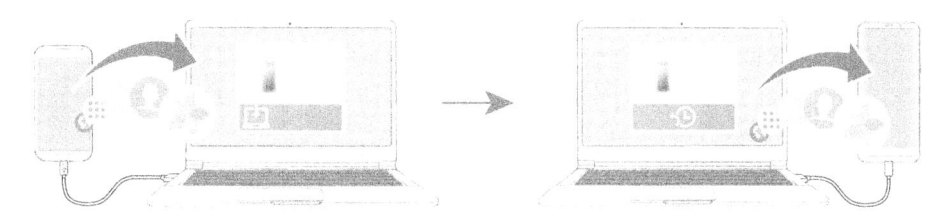

1 On the computer, visit www.samsung.com/smartswitch to download Smart Switch.

2 On the computer, launch Smart Switch.

　　If your previous device is not a Samsung device, back up data to a computer using a program provided by the device's manufacturer. Then, skip to the fifth step.

3 Connect your previous device to the computer using the device's USB cable.

4 On the computer, follow the on-screen instructions to back up data from the device. Then, disconnect your previous device from the computer.

5 Connect your device to the computer using the USB cable.

6 On the computer, follow the on-screen instructions to transfer data to your device.

Viewing imported data

You can view the imported data on the same app from your previous device.

If your new device does not have the same apps to view or play the imported data, the data will be saved to a similar app.

Understanding the screen

Controlling the touchscreen

- Do not allow the touchscreen to come into contact with other electrical devices. Electrostatic discharges can cause the touchscreen to malfunction.
- To avoid damaging the touchscreen, do not tap it with anything sharp or apply excessive pressure to it with your fingertips.
- It is recommended not to use fixed graphics on part or all of the touchscreen for extended periods. Doing so may result in afterimages (screen burn-in) or ghosting.

- The device may not recognise touch inputs close to the edges of the screen, which are outside of the touch input area.
- It is recommended to use fingers when you use the touchscreen.

Tapping

Tap the screen.

Tapping and holding

Tap and hold the screen for approximately 2 seconds.

Basics

Dragging

Tap and hold an item and drag it to the target position.

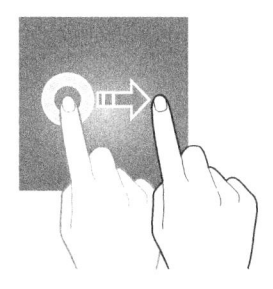

Double-tapping

Double-tap the screen.

Swiping

Swipe upwards, downwards, to the left, or to the right.

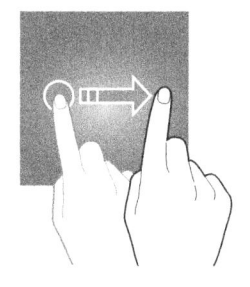

Spreading and pinching

Spread two fingers apart or pinch on the screen.

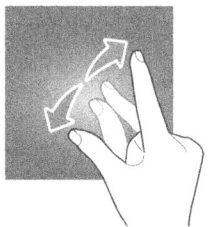

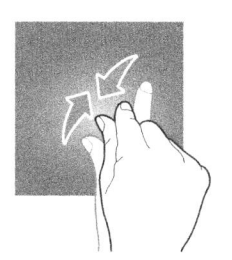

Basics

Navigation bar (soft buttons)

When you turn on the screen, the soft buttons will appear on the navigation bar at the bottom of the screen. The soft buttons are set to the Recents button, Home button, and Back button by default. The functions of the buttons can change according to the app currently being used or usage environment.

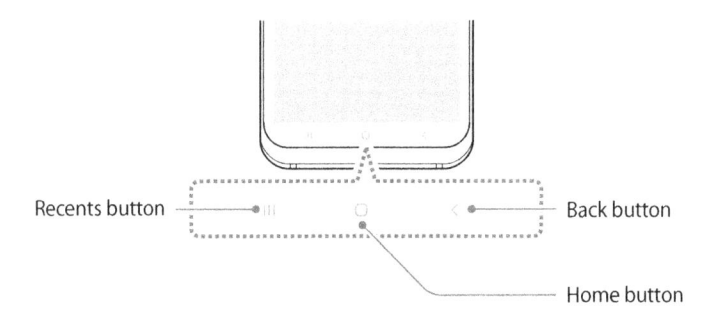

Recents button — Back button

Home button

Button		Function
|||	Recents	• Tap to open the list of recent apps.
○	Home	• Tap to return to the Home screen. • Tap and hold to launch the **Google Assistant** app.
<	Back	• Tap to return to the previous screen.

Basics

Hiding the navigation bar

View files or use apps on a wider screen by hiding the navigation bar.

Launch the **Settings** app, tap **Display** → **Navigation bar**, and then tap **Full screen gestures** under **Navigation type**. The navigation bar will be hidden and the gesture hints will appear where the soft buttons are located. To use the soft buttons, drag the gesture hint of the desired button upwards.

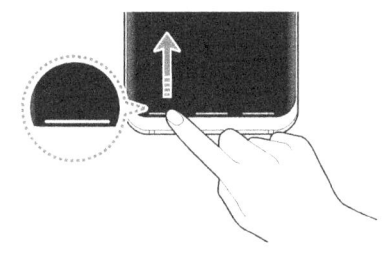

If you want to hide the gesture hints at the bottom of the screen, tap the **Gesture hints** switch to deactivate it.

Turning on the screen using the Home button

Hard press the Home button or the Home button area to turn on the screen.

On the Always On Display, you can also turn on the screen by double-tapping the Home button.

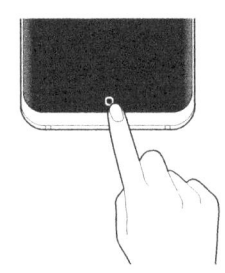

Basics

Setting the navigation bar

Launch the **Settings** app, tap **Display** → **Navigation bar**, and then select an option.

- **Hard press Home button**: Set the device to return to the Home screen when you hard press the Home button. You can also adjust the amount of pressure needed to use the Home button when hard pressing it.
- **Unlock with Home button**: Set the device to unlock the screen without swiping on the locked screen when you hard press the Home button. This feature is available when **Hard press Home button** is activated.
- **Navigation type**: Set the device to hide or display the navigation bar. To hide the navigation bar, tap **Full screen gestures**. While the navigation bar is hidden, you can use the soft buttons by dragging the gesture hint of the desired button upwards.
- **Button order**: Change the order of the buttons on the navigation bar.
- **Gesture hints**: Set the device to display indicators at the bottom of the screen to show where the soft buttons are located. This feature appears only when you select **Full screen gestures**.

Basics

Home screen and Apps screen

The Home screen is the starting point for accessing all of the device's features. It displays widgets, shortcuts to apps, and more.

The Apps screen displays icons for all apps, including newly installed apps.

The screen may appear differently depending on the region or service provider.

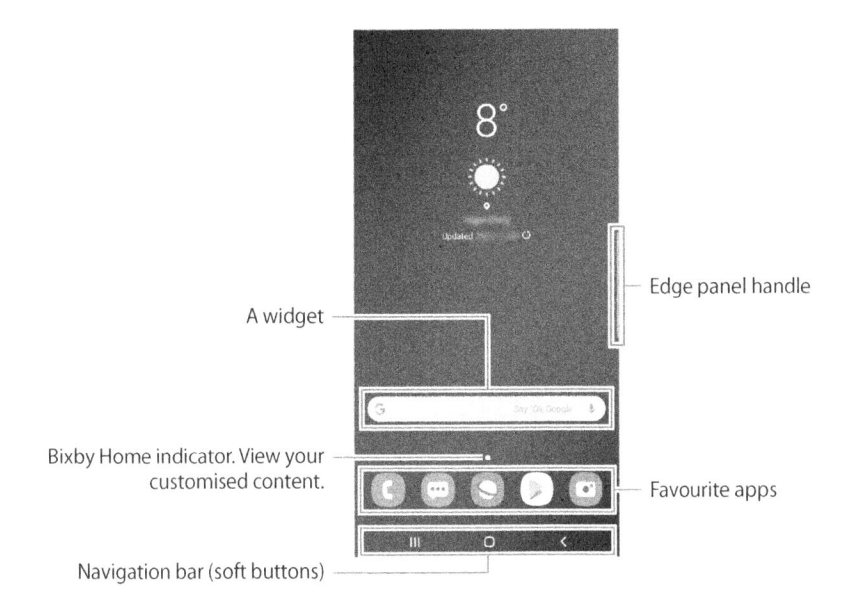

A widget

Edge panel handle

Bixby Home indicator. View your customised content.

Favourite apps

Navigation bar (soft buttons)

Basics

Switching between Home and Apps screens

On the Home screen, swipe upwards or downwards to open the Apps screen.

To return to the Home screen, swipe upwards or downwards on the Apps screen. Alternatively, tap the Home button or the Back button.

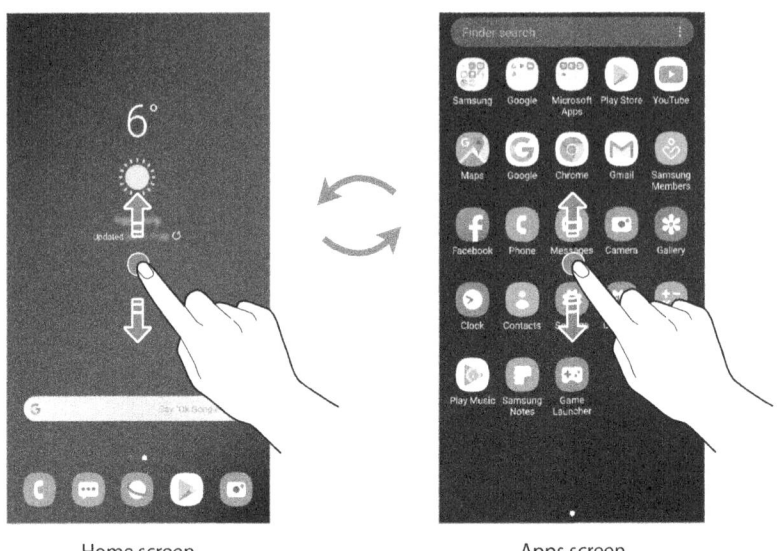

Home screen Apps screen

If you add the Apps button on the Home screen, you can open the Apps screen by tapping the button. On the Home screen, tap and hold an empty area, tap **Home screen settings**, and then tap the **Apps button** switch to activate it. The Apps button will be added at the bottom of the Home screen.

Apps button

Basics

Display the screen in landscape mode

On the Home screen, tap and hold an empty area, tap **Home screen settings**, and then tap the **Portrait mode only** switch to deactivate it.

Rotate the device until it is horizontal to view the screen in landscape mode.

Moving items

Tap and hold an item, and then drag it to a new location. To move the item to another panel, drag it to the side of the screen.

To add a shortcut to an app on the Home screen, tap and hold an item on the Apps screen, and then drag it to the top of the screen. A shortcut to the app will be added on the Home screen.

You can also move frequently used apps to the shortcuts area at the bottom of the Home screen.

Basics

Creating folders

Create folders and gather similar apps to quickly access and launch apps.

On the Home screen or the Apps screen, tap and hold an app, and then drag it over another app.

A new folder containing the selected apps will be created. Tap **Enter folder name** and enter a folder name.

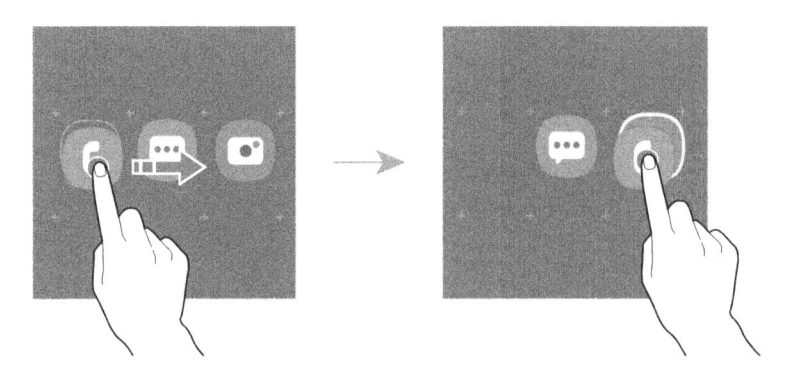

- **Adding more apps**

  Tap **Add apps** on the folder. Tick the apps to add and tap **Add**. You can also add an app by dragging it to the folder.

- **Moving apps from a folder**

  Tap and hold an app to drag it to a new location.

- **Deleting a folder**

  Tap and hold a folder, and then tap **Delete folder**. Only the folder will be deleted. The folder's apps will be relocated to the Apps screen.

Basics

Editing the Home screen

On the Home screen, tap and hold an empty area, or pinch your fingers together to access the editing options. You can set the wallpaper, add widgets, and more. You can also add, delete, or rearrange Home screen panels.

- Adding panels: Swipe to the left, and then tap ⊕.
- Moving panels: Tap and hold a panel preview, and then drag it to a new location.
- Deleting panels: Tap 🗑 on the panel.

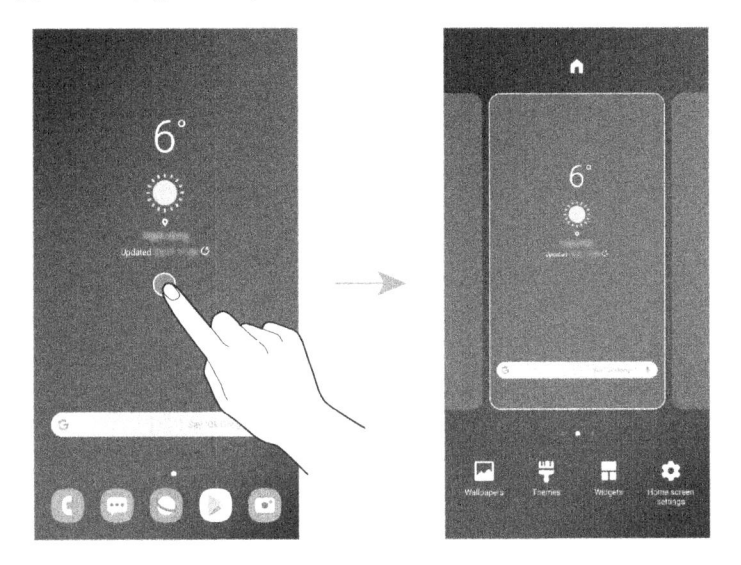

- **Wallpapers**: Change the wallpaper settings for the Home screen and the locked screen.
- **Themes**: Change the device's theme. Visual elements of interface, such as colours, icons, and wallpapers, will change depending on the selected theme.
- **Widgets**: Widgets are small apps that launch specific app functions to provide information and convenient access on your Home screen. Tap and hold a widget, and then drag it to the Home screen. The widget will be added on the Home screen.
- **Home screen settings**: Change the size of the grid to display more or fewer items on the Home screen and more.

Basics

Displaying all apps on the Home screen

Without using a separate Apps screen, you can set the device to display all apps on the Home screen. On the Home screen, tap and hold an empty area, and then tap **Home screen settings** → **Home screen layout** → **Home screen only** → **Apply**.

You can now access all your apps by swiping to the left on the Home screen.

Indicator icons

Indicator icons appear on the status bar at the top of the screen. The icons listed in the table below are most common.

- The status bar may not appear at the top of the screen in some apps. To display the status bar, drag down from the top of the screen.
- Some indicator icons appear only when you open the notification panel.

Icon	Meaning
⊘	No signal
▁▃▅	Signal strength
R▁▃▅	Roaming (outside of normal service area)
G↕	GPRS network connected
E↕	EDGE network connected
3G↕	UMTS network connected
H↕	HSDPA network connected
H+↕	HSPA+ network connected
4G↕ / LTE↕	LTE network connected (LTE-enabled models)
📶	Wi-Fi connected
✷	Bluetooth feature activated
⦿	Location services being used
📞	Call in progress
⤵	Missed call

Basics

Icon	Meaning
	New text or multimedia message
	Alarm activated
	Mute mode activated
	Vibration mode activated
	Flight mode activated
	Error occurred or caution required
	Battery charging
	Battery power level

Lock screen

Pressing the Power key turns off the screen and locks it. Also, the screen turns off and automatically locks if the device is not used for a specified period.

To unlock the screen, swipe in any direction when the screen turns on.

If the screen is off, press the Power key or hard press the Home button or the Home button area to turn on the screen.

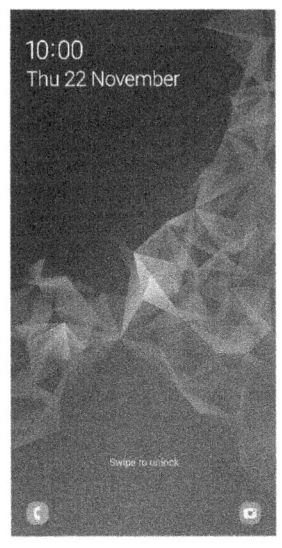

Locked screen

Basics

Changing the screen lock method

To change the screen lock method, launch the **Settings** app, tap **Lock screen** → **Screen lock type**, and then select a method.

When you set a pattern, PIN, password, face, iris, or fingerprint for the screen lock method, you can protect your personal information by preventing others from accessing your device. After setting the screen lock method, the device will require an unlock code whenever unlocking it.

- **Swipe**: Swipe in any direction on the screen to unlock it.
- **Pattern**: Draw a pattern with four or more dots to unlock the screen.
- **PIN**: Enter a PIN with at least four numbers to unlock the screen.
- **Password**: Enter a password with at least four characters, numbers, or symbols to unlock the screen.
- **None**: Do not set a screen lock method.
- **Intelligent Scan**: Register both your face and irises to the device to unlock the screen more conveniently. Refer to Intelligent Scan for more information.
- **Face**: Register your face to unlock the screen. Refer to Face recognition for more information.
- **Iris**: Register your irises to unlock the screen. Refer to Iris recognition for more information.
- **Fingerprints**: Register your fingerprints to unlock the screen. Refer to Fingerprint recognition for more information.

You can set your device to perform a factory data reset if you enter the unlock code incorrectly several times in a row and reach the attempt limit. Launch the **Settings** app, tap **Lock screen** → **Secure lock settings**, unlock the screen using the preset screen lock method, and then tap the **Auto factory reset** switch to activate it.

Basics

Screen capture

Capture a screenshot while using the device and write on, draw on, crop, or share the captured screen. You can capture the current screen and scrollable area.

Use the following methods to capture a screenshot. Captured screenshots will be saved in **Gallery**.

- Key capture: Press and hold the Volume Down key and the Power key simultaneously.
- Swipe capture: Swipe your hand to the left or right across the screen.

- It is not possible to capture a screenshot while using some apps and features.
- If capturing a screenshot by swiping is not activated, launch the **Settings** app, tap **Advanced features** → **Motions and gestures**, and then tap the **Palm swipe to capture** switch to activate it.

After capturing a screenshot, use the following options on the toolbar at the bottom of the screen:

- : Capture the current content and the hidden content on an elongated page, such as a webpage. When you tap , the screen will automatically scroll down and more content will be captured.
- : Crop a portion from the screenshot. The cropped area will be saved in **Gallery**.
- : Write or draw on the screenshot.
- : Share the screenshot with others.

If the options are not visible on the captured screen, launch the **Settings** app, tap **Advanced features**, and then tap the **Smart capture** switch to activate it.

Basics

Notification panel

When you receive new notifications, such as messages or missed calls, indicator icons appear on the status bar. To see more information about the icons, open the notification panel and view the details.

To open the notification panel, drag the status bar downwards. To close the notification panel, swipe upwards on the screen.

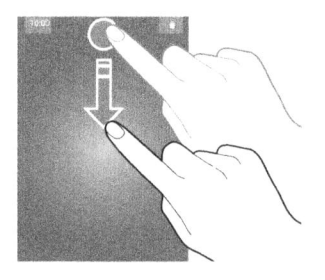

You can use the following functions on the notification panel.

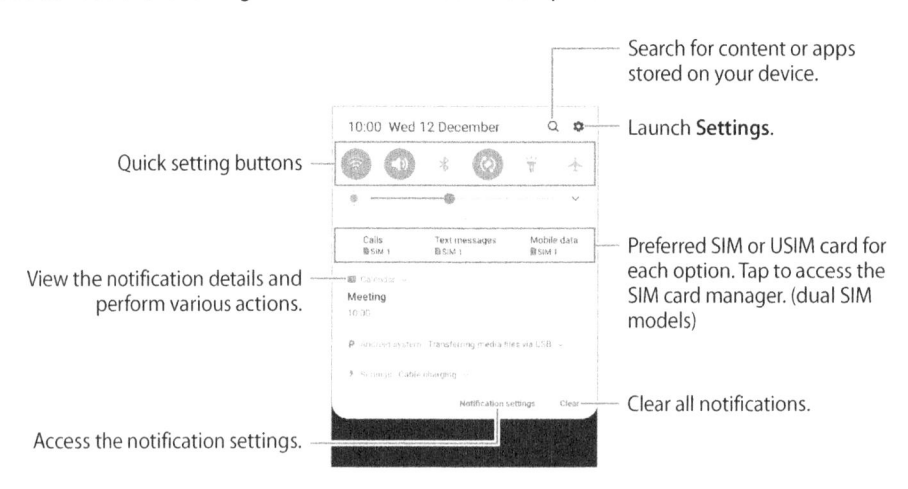

Quick setting buttons

View the notification details and perform various actions.

Access the notification settings.

Search for content or apps stored on your device.

Launch **Settings**.

Preferred SIM or USIM card for each option. Tap to access the SIM card manager. (dual SIM models)

Clear all notifications.

56

Basics

Using quick setting buttons

Tap quick setting buttons to activate certain features. Swipe downwards on the notification panel to view more buttons.

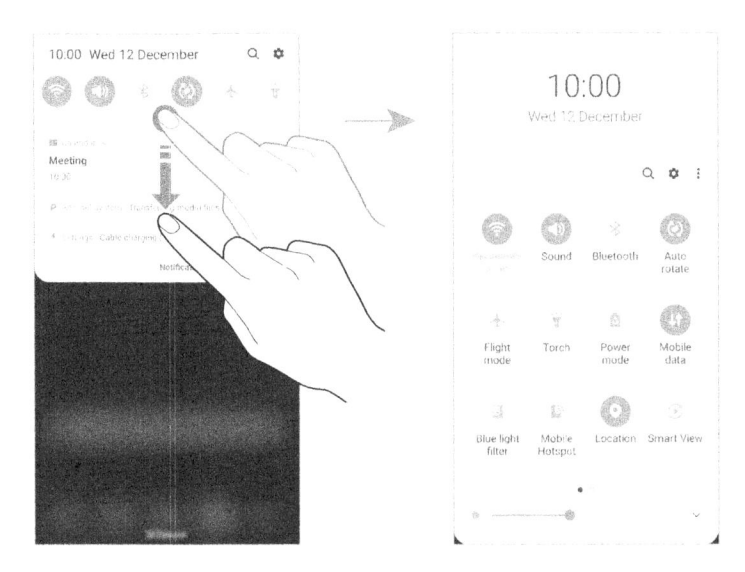

To change feature settings, tap the text under each button. To view more detailed settings, tap and hold a button.

To rearrange buttons, tap ⋮ → **Button order**, tap and hold a button, and then drag it to another location.

Basics

Entering text

Keyboard layout

A keyboard appears automatically when you enter text to send messages, create notes, and more.

> Text entry is not supported in some languages. To enter text, you must change the input language to one of the supported languages.

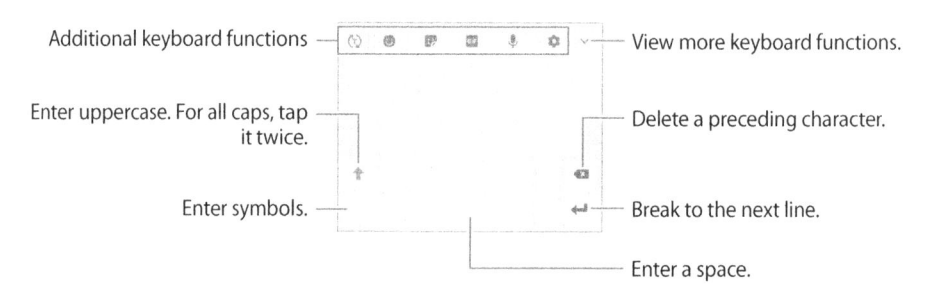

Additional keyboard functions — View more keyboard functions.

Enter uppercase. For all caps, tap it twice. — Delete a preceding character.

Enter symbols. — Break to the next line.

Enter a space.

Changing the input language

Tap ✿ → **Languages and types** → **Manage input languages**, and then select the languages to use. When you select two or more languages, you can switch between the input languages by swiping to the left or right on the space key.

Basics

Changing the keyboard

Tap ⌨ to change the keyboard.

To change the keyboard type, tap ⚙ → **Languages and types**, select a language, and then select the keyboard type you want.

- If the keyboard button (⌨) does not appear on the navigation bar, launch the **Settings** app, tap **General management** → **Language and input**, and then tap the **Show Keyboard button** switch to activate it.
- On a **3x4 keyboard**, a key has three or four characters. To enter a character, tap the corresponding key repeatedly until the desired character appears.

Additional keyboard functions

- 🔮 : Predict words based on your input and show word suggestions. To return to the keyboard functions list, tap 🙂.
- 😊 : Enter emoticons.
- 🗟 : Enter stickers. You can also enter My Emoji stickers that look like you. Refer to Enjoying My Emoji stickers while chatting for more information.
- GIF : Attach animated GIFs.

This feature may not be available depending on the region or service provider.

- 🎤 : Enter text by voice.
- ⚙ : Change the keyboard settings.
- ⌄ → 📋 : Add an item from the clipboard.
- ⌄ → ⌨ : Change the keyboard mode or size.

Basics

Copying and pasting

1 Tap and hold over text.

2 Drag ● or ● to select the desired text, or tap **Select all** to select all text.

3 Tap **Copy** or **Cut**.
   The selected text is copied to the clipboard.

4 Tap and hold where the text is to be inserted and tap **Paste**.
   To paste text that you have previously copied, tap **Clipboard** and select the text.

Dictionary

Look up definitions for words while using certain features, such as when browsing webpages.

1 Tap and hold over a word that you want to look up.
   If the word you want to look up is not selected, drag ● or ● to select the desired text.

2 Tap ⋮ → **Dictionary** on the options list.
   If a dictionary is not preinstalled on the device, tap **Move to Manage dictionaries**, tap ● next to a dictionary, and then tap **INSTALL** to download it.

3 View the definition in the dictionary pop-up window.
   To switch to the full screen view, tap ⬈. Tap the definition on the screen to view more definitions. In the detailed view, tap ★ to add the word to your favourite words list or tap **Search Web** to use the word as a search term.

Apps and features

Installing or uninstalling apps

Galaxy Apps

Purchase and download apps. You can download apps that are specialised for Samsung Galaxy devices.

Open the **Samsung** folder and launch the **Galaxy Apps** app.

This app may not be available depending on the region or service provider.

Installing apps

Browse apps by category or tap the search field to search for a keyword.

Select an app to view information about it. To download free apps, tap **INSTALL**. To purchase and download apps where charges apply, tap the price and follow the on-screen instructions.

To change the auto update settings, tap → **Settings** → **Auto update apps**, and then select an option.

Play Store

Purchase and download apps.

Launch the **Play Store** app.

Installing apps

Browse apps by category or search for apps by keyword.

Select an app to view information about it. To download free apps, tap **INSTALL**. To purchase and download apps where charges apply, tap the price and follow the on-screen instructions.

To change the auto update settings, tap → **Settings** → **Auto-update apps**, and then select an option.

Managing apps

Uninstalling or disabling apps

Tap and hold an app and select an option.

- **Disable**: Disable selected default apps that cannot be uninstalled from the device.
- **Uninstall**: Uninstall downloaded apps.

Enabling apps

Launch the **Settings** app, tap **Apps** → ▼ → **Disabled**, select an app, and then tap **Enable**.

Setting app permissions

For some apps to operate properly, they may need permission to access or use information on your device. When you open an app, a pop-up window may appear and request access to certain features or information. Tap **Allow** on the pop-up window to grant permissions to the app.

To view your app permission settings, launch the **Settings** app and tap **Apps**. Select an app and tap **Permissions**. You can view the app's permissions list and change its permissions.

To view or change app permission settings by permission category, launch the **Settings** app and tap **Apps** → ⋮ → **App permissions** → **Permissions**. Select an item and tap the switches next to apps to grant permissions.

If you do not grant permissions to apps, the basic features of the apps may not function properly.

Apps and features

Bixby

Introduction

Bixby is an intelligent voice service that helps you use the device more conveniently.

You can talk to Bixby or type text. Bixby will launch a function you request or show the information you want. It also learns your usage patterns and environments. The more it learns about you, the more precisely it will understand you.

- To use Bixby, your device must be connected to a Wi-Fi or mobile network.
- To use Bixby, you must register and sign in to your Samsung account.
- Bixby is only available in some languages, and certain features may not be available depending on your region.

Starting Bixby

When you launch Bixby for the first time, the Bixby intro page will appear. You must select the language to use with Bixby, register and sign in to your Samsung account according to the on-screen instructions, and then agree to the terms and conditions.

1 Press the Bixby key.

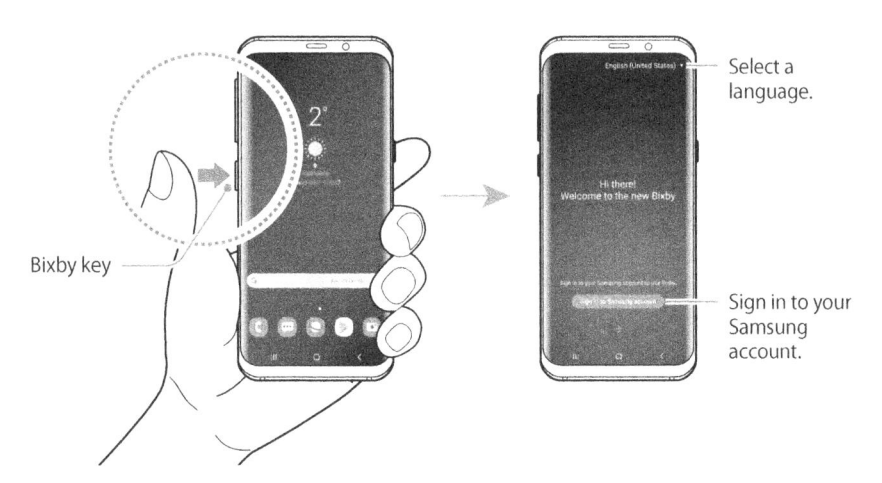

Bixby key

Select a language.

Sign in to your Samsung account.

Apps and features

2 Select the language to use with Bixby.

3 Tap **Sign in to Samsung account** and follow the on-screen instructions to sign in to your Samsung account.

> If you are already signed in, your account information will appear on the screen.

4 Tap ⊙.

5 Read and agree to the terms and conditions and tap ⊙.

6 Tap ⊙ and follow the on-screen instructions to register your voice.

If you set the voice wake-up feature, you can start a conversation with Bixby by saying "Hi, Bixby".

7 Tap ⊙ to complete the setup.

The Bixby screen will appear.

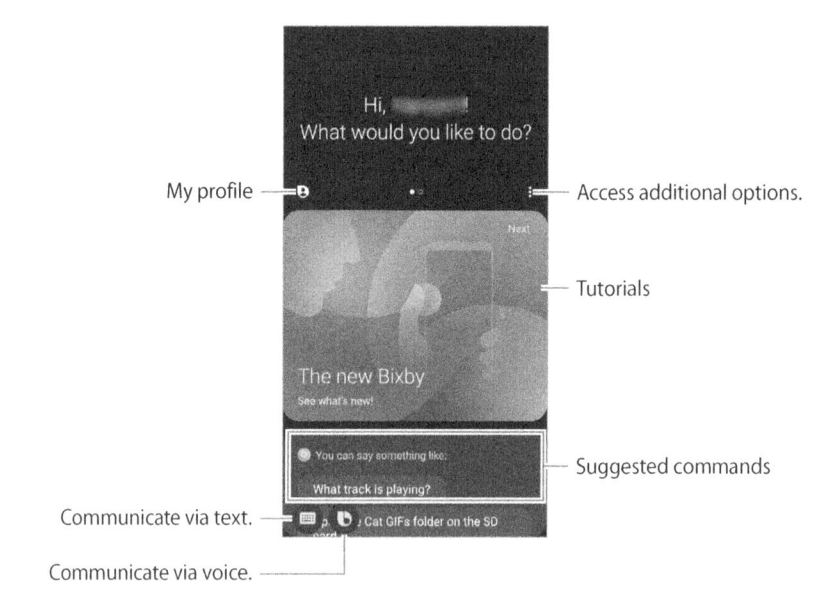

- My profile
- Access additional options.
- Tutorials
- Suggested commands
- Communicate via text.
- Communicate via voice.

Apps and features

Using Bixby

When you say what you want to Bixby, Bixby will launch corresponding functions or show the information you requested.

While pressing and holding the Bixby key, say what you want to Bixby, and then release your finger from the key when you are finished speaking. Alternatively, say "Hi, Bixby", and when the device emits a sound, say what you want.

For example, while pressing and holding the Bixby key, say "How's the weather today?" The weather information will appear on the screen.

If you want to know the weather tomorrow, while pressing and holding the Bixby key, just say "Tomorrow?" Because Bixby understands the context of the conversation, it will show you tomorrow's weather.

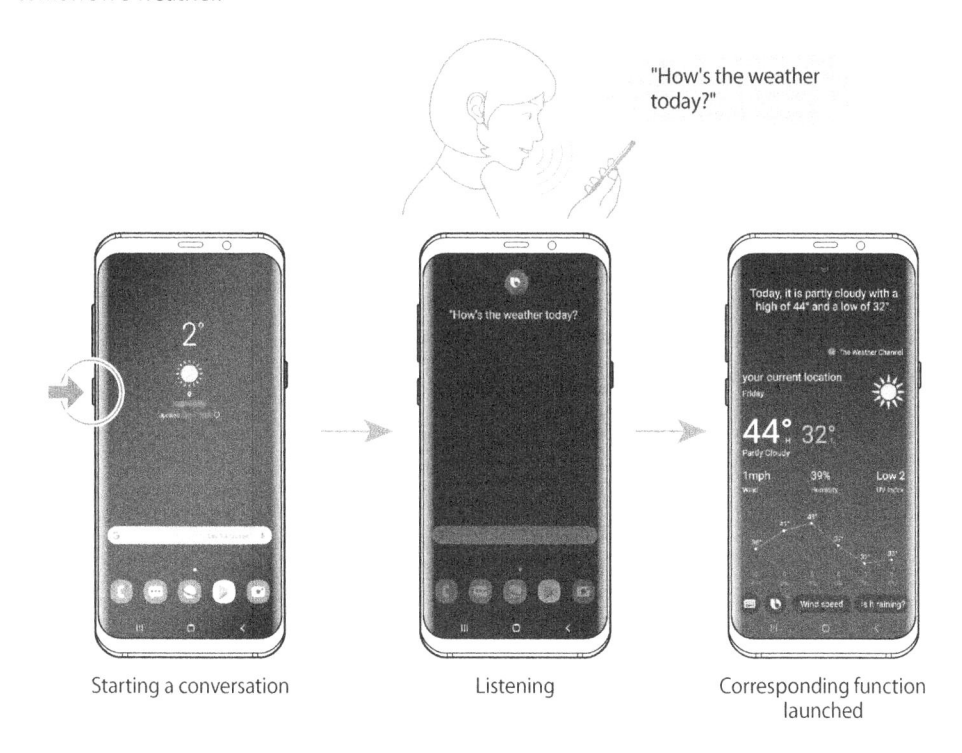

"How's the weather today?"

Starting a conversation   Listening   Corresponding function launched

Apps and features

If Bixby asks you a question during a conversation, while pressing and holding the Bixby key, answer Bixby. Or, tap and answer Bixby.

If you are using headphones or Bluetooth audio, or start a conversation by saying "Hi, Bixby", you can continue the conversation without tapping the icon. Press the Bixby key and tap → **Settings** → **Automatic listening** → **Hands-free only**.

Waking up Bixby using your voice

You can start a conversation with Bixby by saying "Hi, Bixby". Register your voice so that Bixby will respond to your voice when you say "Hi, Bixby".

1 Press the Bixby key and tap → **Settings** → **Voice wake-up**.

2 Tap the **Wake with "Hi, Bixby"** switch to activate it.

3 Follow the on-screen instructions to complete the setup.

Now you can say "Hi, Bixby", and when the device emits a sound, start a conversation.

Communicating by typing text

If your voice is not recognised due to noisy environments or if you are in a situation where speaking is difficult, you can communicate with Bixby via text.

Press the Bixby key, tap , and then type what you want.

During the communication, Bixby also will answer you through text instead of voice feedback.

Bixby usages

Launching apps or services

You can launch features quickly via Bixby. You can also use various convenient services, such as ordering coffee or searching for nearby restaurants or hotels and making a reservation.

For example, while pressing and holding the Bixby key, say "Call mom", and then release your finger from the Bixby key. Bixby will now make a call to the contact saved as mom.

Viewing more ways to use Bixby

To view more ways to use Bixby, press the Bixby key, and then swipe to the left on the screen. You can check out services supported by Bixby and examples of commands.

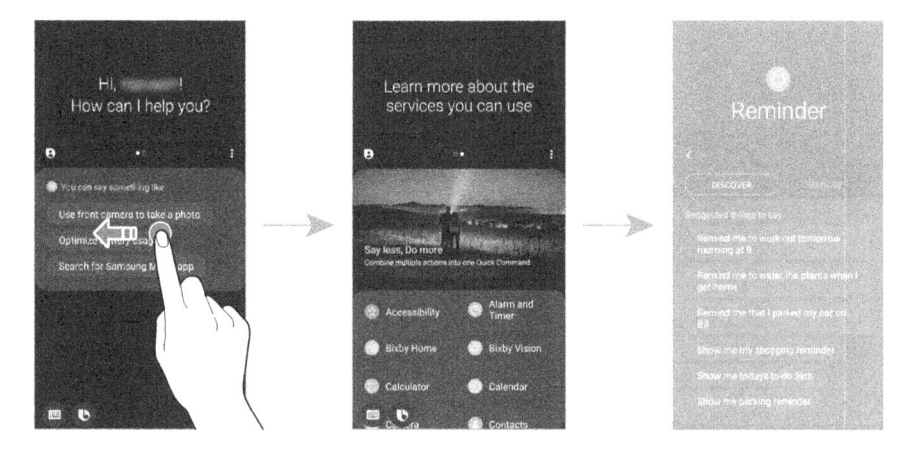

Some features may not be available depending on the region or service provider.

Apps and features

Additional Bixby functions

Waking up Bixby while using the speaker

You can wake up Bixby by saying "Hi, Bixby" even when the speaker plays alarms, ringtone, or media.

Press the Bixby key, tap ⋮ → **Settings** → **Voice wake-up**, and then tap the **Use when phone speaker playing** switch to activate it.

Checking what Bixby understood

You can check how Bixby understood what you said. If Bixby understood your intention differently, you can let Bixby know the correct meaning.

Drag Bixby's answer area downwards. What Bixby understood and any used services will appear. If Bixby misunderstood your intention, edit the content and change the app or service to use.

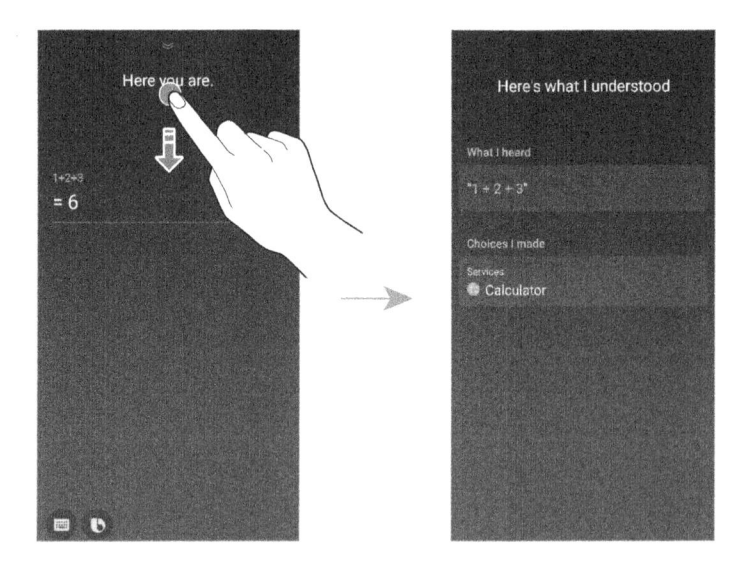

Apps and features

Using quick commands

You can add quick commands so that you can give commands more quickly and easily. You can also give multiple commands together by adding them to a quick command.

1 Press the Bixby key and tap 😊 → **Quick commands** → ➕.

2 Tap **Quick command word or phrase** and enter a quick command name.

3 Tap **Add a command** and select a method you want.
 • **Select a command**: Select one from the commands list.
 • **Say a command**: Say your command.
 • **Type a command**: Type your command.

4 Select or enter a command that Bixby will perform.
 To add additional commands, tap **Add a command**.

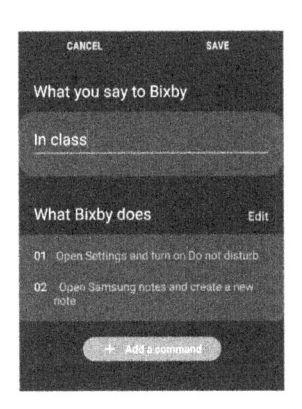

5 Tap **SAVE**.
 Now you can give multiple commands by saying the quick commands you added.

69

Apps and features

Using earphones or a Bluetooth headset

Connect earphones or a Bluetooth headset to the device when your voice is not heard clearly via the built-in microphone due to noisy environments. Press and hold the Call button on earphones or a Bluetooth headset to launch Bixby and say your request to the microphone.

This feature may not be available or its method of use may vary depending on the earphones and Bluetooth headset.

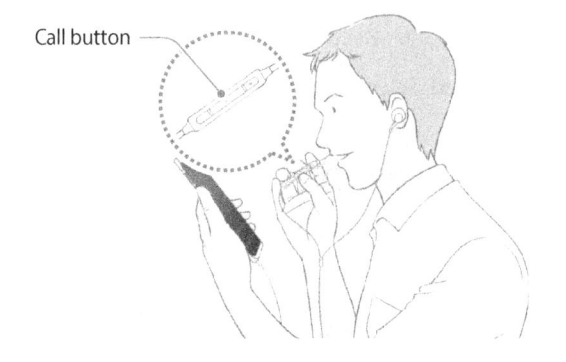

Call button

Apps and features

Customising the Bixby settings

Press the Bixby key and tap ⋮ → **Settings**.

- **Language and voice style**: Set the language to communicate with Bixby and set the style of voice feedback. The selected language is applied only when you talk with Bixby.

    > Bixby is only available in some languages, and certain features may not be available depending on your region. To see the list of supported languages, tap **Language**.

- **Voice response**: Change the voice feedback settings for Bixby.
- **Automatic listening**: Set Bixby to automatically listen when it asks a question so you can respond without pressing the icon. This option is available only if you are using headphones or Bluetooth audio, or start a conversation by saying "Hi, Bixby".
- **Voice wake-up**: Set Bixby to wake up when it hears you say "Hi, Bixby". You can also change the settings for the voice wake-up feature.
- **Use while phone locked**: Set Bixby to complete some actions, such as making a call or launching a map app, while the device is locked.
- **Bixby key**: Select how many times you must press the Bixby key to open the Bixby screen.
- **Marketing notifications**: Set to receive notifications about marketing information.
- **Privacy**: Set to use Bixby's interactive and customised services to enhance your experience.
- **About Bixby Voice**: View the Bixby version and legal information.

Apps and features

Bixby Vision

Bixby Vision is a service that provides information, such as similar images, location, translated text, and QR codes. Bixby Vision recognises objects quickly and intuitively even when you do not know its name.

Use the following Bixby Vision features.

Text   Place   QR code
   Image   Wine

- To use this feature, the device must be connected to a Wi-Fi or mobile network.
- To use this feature, you must register and sign in to your Samsung account.
- The available features and search results may vary depending on the region or service provider.
- This feature may not be available or you may not get correct search results depending on the image size, format, or resolution.
- Samsung is not responsible for the product information provided by Bixby Vision.

Apps and features

Launching Bixby Vision

1 Launch Bixby Vision using one of these methods.

- In the **Camera** app, tap **Bixby Vision**.
- In the **Gallery** app, select an image and tap .
- In the **Internet** app, tap and hold an image and tap **Bixby Vision**.
- If you added the Bixby Vision app icon to the Home screen and Apps screen, launch the **Bixby Vision** app.

2 Select the feature you want.

3 Keep the object within the screen to recognise it.

When the object is recognised, search results will appear on the screen.

To view more information, tap the feature icon or select a search result.

Translating or extracting text

Recognise and show the translated text on the screen. You can also extract text from a document or an image file.

For example, if you want to know what a sign says while travelling abroad, use the Bixby Vision features. The device will translate the sign's text into the language you select.

1 When you have a desired image or object, launch Bixby Vision.

2 Select and keep the text within the screen to recognise it.

The translated text will appear on the screen.

- To extract text, tap . You can share or save the extracted text.
- To change the source or target language, tap the language settings panel at the top of the screen.

Apps and features

Searching for similar images

Search for images similar to the recognised object online. You can view various images with properties similar to the object, such as colour or shape.

For example, if you want to know the title of a photo or image, use the Bixby Vision features. The device will search for and show you related information or images with similar characteristics.

1 When you have a desired image or object, launch Bixby Vision.

2 Select and keep the object within the screen to recognise it.

3 Tap or select a search result on the screen.
   The similar images will appear.

Searching for nearby places

Search for information about nearby places by recognising your current location.

For example, if you want to search for nearby cafes, use the Bixby Vision features. The device will search for and show you nearby cafes.

1 When you have a desired place or object, launch Bixby Vision.

2 Select and keep the place or object within the screen to recognise it.
   You can view basic information about nearby places.
   If you want to search for places in another direction, point the camera towards the direction.

   If you are using Bixby Vision with the camera, you can view your current location and weather information. To view your current location on the map, point the camera towards the ground. To view the current weather information, point the camera towards the sky.

3 Tap or select a search result on the screen.
   The device will show information of nearby places.

Apps and features

Searching for wine information

Detect the information from a wine label and search for information on the wine.

For example, if you find your favourite wine or want to know more about a wine, use the Bixby Vision features.

1 When you have a desired image or object, launch Bixby Vision.

2 Select and keep the wine label within the screen to recognise it.

3 Tap or select a search result on the screen.
   The information about the wine label will appear.

Reading QR codes

Recognise QR codes and view a variety of information, such as websites, photos, videos, maps, and business cards.

1 When you have a desired image or object, launch Bixby Vision.

2 Select and keep the QR code within the screen to recognise it.
   The information connected to the QR code will appear.

Downloading additional features

You can download various Bixby Vision features.

On the Bixby Vision screen, tap → **ADD** and download apps or features.

Apps and features

Bixby Home

On the Bixby Home screen, you can view recommended services and information that Bixby provides by analysing your usage patterns and your routine.

- To view more content, connect to a Wi-Fi or mobile network.
- To fully use this feature, you must register and sign in to your Samsung account.

Opening Bixby Home

1 On the Home screen, swipe to the right.

   The Bixby Home screen will appear.

   When launching this feature for the first time or after performing a data reset, follow the on-screen instructions to complete the setup.

2 Swipe upwards or downwards to view recommended content.

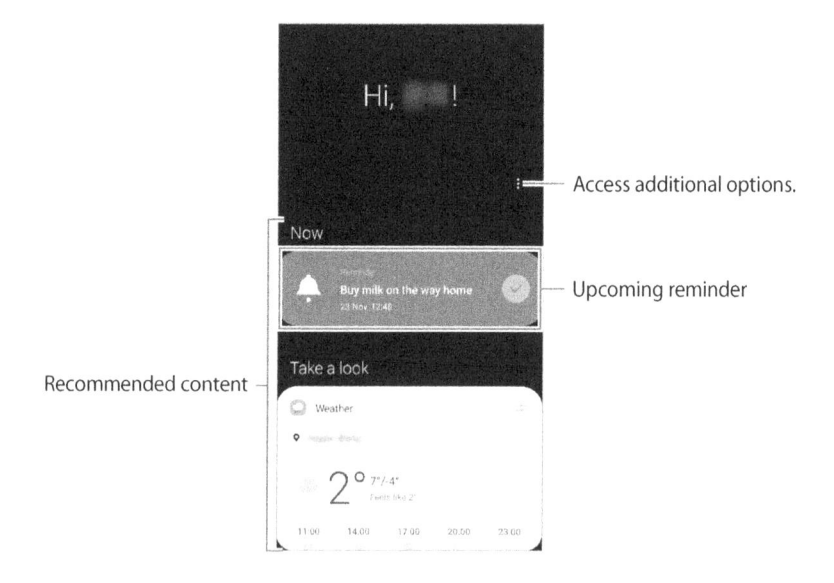

Access additional options.

Upcoming reminder

Recommended content

3 To close Bixby Home, swipe to the left on the screen or tap the Back button.

Apps and features

Using recommended content on Bixby Home

When you open Bixby Home, you can view the content that is frequently updated as cards. Swipe upwards or downwards to view the cards.

For example, on the way to the office in the morning, you can view your day's schedule and play your favourite music on the Bixby Home screen. In the evening, you can view alarms, check your daily activity, and view your friends' feeds.

> The content and order of the cards update automatically at a specified interval. To manually update cards, swipe downwards on the screen.

Editing cards list

- To pin a card to the top of the Bixby Home screen, tap → **Pin to top**. To unpin a card, tap → **Unpin**.
- To stop displaying a card on the list, drag the card to the right and tap **Don't show again**.
- To hide a card from the list, drag the card to the right and tap **Hide for now**.

Selecting apps to show as cards

Add or delete apps to show as cards on the Bixby Home screen.

On the Bixby Home screen, tap → **Cards** and tap the switches next to items to add or delete them.

> If an app is not installed on the device, you must install it to use it. On the Bixby Home screen, tap → **Cards** and then download an app.

Customising the Bixby Home settings

On the Bixby Home screen, tap → **Settings**.

- **Customisation Service**: Set to use Bixby's interactive and customised services to enhance your experience.
- **Bixby Home content providers**: Read and agree to or withdraw your agreement from the terms and conditions and privacy policies of each content provider.
- **About Bixby Home**: View the Bixby Home version and legal information.

Apps and features

Reminder

Create reminders to schedule to-do items or to view content later. You will receive notifications at the preset time or location for each reminder.

- To receive more accurate notifications, connect to a Wi-Fi or mobile network.
- To fully use this feature, you must register and sign in to your Samsung account.
- To use location reminders, the GPS feature must be activated.

Starting Reminder

You can start Reminder from Bixby Home.

1 On the Home screen, swipe to the right.

The Bixby Home screen will appear.

2 Tap **Get started** on the **Reminder** card.

The Reminder screen will appear and the **Reminder** app icon ( ) will be added to the Apps screen.

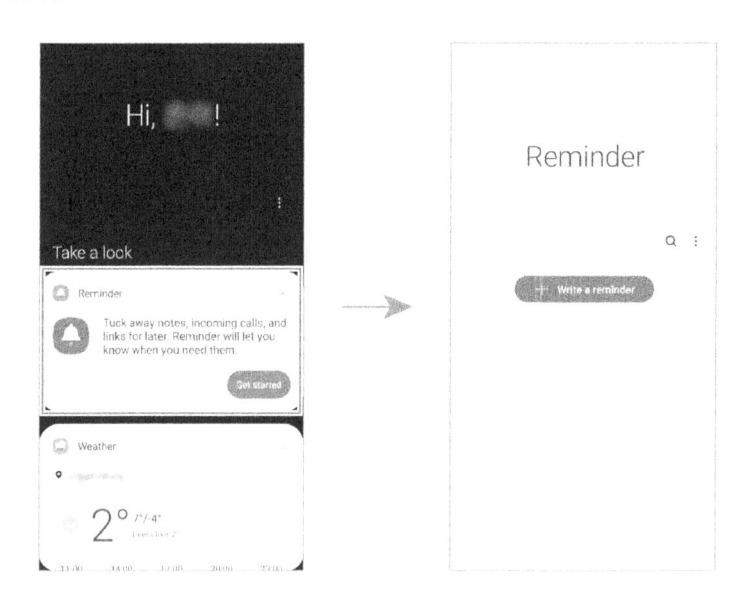

Apps and features

Creating reminders

Create reminders with various methods. Reminder will alert you if you create a reminder with a specified time or location setting. You can also save various content, such as a single memo or webpage address, and view it later.

For example, create a reminder to alert you to 'Water the flowers when I get home'.

1 Launch the **Reminder** app.

2 Tap **Write a reminder** or ╋ and enter 'Water the flowers'.

3 Tap **Place** → **Set conditions** → **Pick a place** and set the location to home.

4 Tap **When I arrive at** → **Done**.

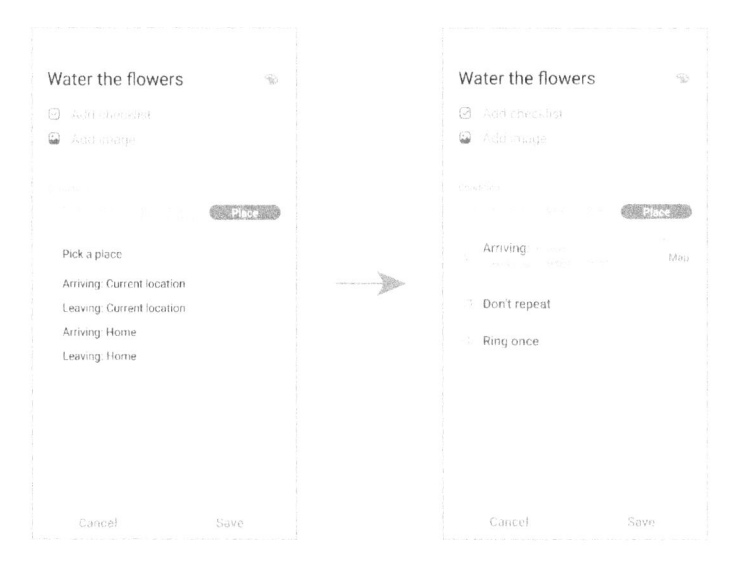

5 Tap **Save** to save the reminder.

When you arrive at home, the 'Water the flowers' notification will appear.

Apps and features

Creating reminders with Bixby

Press and hold the Bixby key and say "Remind me to water the flowers when I get home". Bixby will save what you said as a reminder.

Checking reminder notifications

At the preset time or location, a notification pop-up window will appear. Tap **Complete** or **Snooze**.

Viewing the reminders list

Launch the **Reminder** app to view your reminders list. To view reminder details, select a reminder.

Apps and features

Editing reminder details

Add or edit reminder details, such as frequency, date and time, or location.

1 On the reminders list, select a reminder to edit and tap **Edit**.

2 Edit the conditions and tap **Save**.

Reminder information
Add a checklist.
Add an image.
Change the reminder's colour.
Reminder conditions

Completing reminders

Mark reminders that you do not need to be reminded of as complete.

On the reminders list, select a reminder and tap **Complete**. Alternatively, drag the reminder to the left.

Restoring reminders

Restore reminders that have been completed.

1 On the reminders list, tap ⋮ → **Completed** → **Edit**.

2 Tick items to restore and tap **Restore**.

Reminders will be added to the reminders list and you will be reminded at the preset times.

Deleting reminders

To delete a reminder, drag the reminder to the right. To delete multiple reminders, tap and hold a reminder, tick reminders to delete, and then tap **Delete**.

Apps and features

Phone

Introduction

Make or answer voice and video calls.

Making calls

1 Launch the **Phone** app and tap **Keypad**.

2 Enter a phone number.

3 Tap to make a voice call, or tap to make a video call.

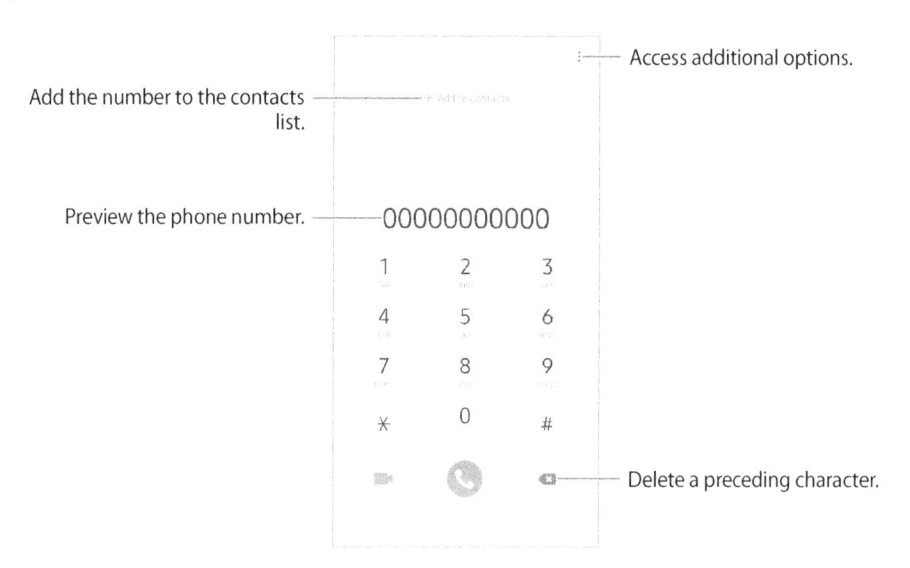

Access additional options.

Add the number to the contacts list.

Preview the phone number. — 00000000000

Delete a preceding character.

Apps and features

Making calls from call logs or contacts list

Tap **Recents** or **Contacts**, and then swipe to the right on a contact or a phone number to make a call.

If this feature is deactivated, launch the **Settings** app, tap **Advanced features** → **Motions and gestures**, and then tap the **Swipe to call or send messages** switch to activate it.

Using speed dial

Set speed dial numbers to quickly make calls.

To set a number to speed dial, tap **Keypad** or **Contacts** → ⋮ → **Speed dial numbers**, select a speed dial number, and then add a phone number.

To make a call, tap and hold a speed dial number on the keypad. For speed dial numbers 10 and up, tap the first digit(s) of the number, and then tap and hold the last digit.

For example, if you set the number **123** as a speed dial number, tap **1**, tap **2**, and then tap and hold **3**.

Making calls from the locked screen

On the locked screen, drag outside the circle.

Making an international call

1. Launch the **Phone** app and tap **Keypad**.
2. Tap and hold **0** until the + sign appears.
3. Enter the country code, area code, and phone number, and then tap .

Apps and features

Receiving calls

Answering a call

When a call comes in, drag ⊙ outside the large circle.

Rejecting a call

When a call comes in, drag ⊙ outside the large circle.

To send a message when rejecting an incoming call, drag the **Send message** bar upwards. If the **Add reminder** switch is activated, a reminder will be saved to alert you of the rejected call one hour later.

To create various rejection messages, launch the **Phone** app, tap ⋮ → **Settings** → **Quick decline messages**, enter a message, and then tap ＋.

Missed calls

If a call is missed, the ✗ icon appears on the status bar. Open the notification panel to view the list of missed calls. Alternatively, launch the **Phone** app and tap **Recents** to view missed calls.

Blocking phone numbers

Block calls from specific numbers added to your block list.

1 Launch the **Phone** app and tap ⋮ → **Settings** → **Block numbers**.

2 Tap **Recents** or **Contacts**, select contacts, and then tap **Done**.

   To manually enter a number, tap **Add phone number**, enter a phone number, and then tap ＋.

When blocked numbers try to contact you, you will not receive notifications. The calls will be logged in the call log.

> You can also block incoming calls from people that do not show their caller ID. Tap the **Block unknown callers** switch to activate the feature.

Apps and features

Options during calls

> If the area around the rear camera and the fingerprint recognition sensor is covered, unwanted noises may incur during a call. Remove accessories, such as a screen protector or stickers, around the rear camera area.

During a voice call

The following actions are available:

- : Access additional options.
- **Add call**: Dial a second call. The first call will be put on hold. When you end the second call, the first call will be resumed.
- **Hold call**: Hold a call. Tap **Resume call** to retrieve the held call.
- **Bluetooth**: Switch to a Bluetooth headset if it is connected to the device.
- **Speaker**: Activate or deactivate the speakerphone. When using the speakerphone, keep the device away from your ears.
- **Mute**: Turn off the microphone so that the other party cannot hear you.
- **Keypad** / **Hide**: Open or close the keypad.
- : End the current call.

During a video call

Tap the screen to use the following options:

- : Access additional options.
- **Camera**: Turn off the camera so that the other party cannot see you.
- **Switch**: Switch between the front and rear cameras.
- : End the current call.
- **Mute**: Turn off the microphone so that the other party cannot hear you.
- **Speaker**: Activate or deactivate the speakerphone. When using the speakerphone, keep the device away from your ears.

Apps and features

Adding a phone number to Contact

Adding a phone number to Contacts from the keypad

1 Launch the **Phone** app and tap **Keypad**.

2 Enter the number.

3 Tap **Add to contacts**.

4 Tap **Add to contacts** to create a new contact, or tap **Update existing** to add the number to an existing contact.

Adding a phone number to Contacts from the calls list

1 Launch the **Phone** app and tap **Recents**.

2 Tap a caller's image and tap **Add**, or tap a phone number and tap **Add to Contacts**.

3 Tap **Add to contacts** to create a new contact, or tap **Update existing** to add the number to an existing contact.

Adding a tag to a phone number

You can add tags to numbers without saving them to Contact. This allows you to view the caller's information when they call without having them listed in Contact.

1 Launch the **Phone** app and tap **Recents**.

2 Tap a phone number → .

3 Tap **Add tag**, enter a tag, and then tap **Add**.

When a call comes from that number, the tag will show under the number.

Apps and features

Contacts

Introduction

Create new contacts or manage contacts on the device.

Adding contacts

Creating a new contact

1 Launch the **Contacts** app and tap .

2 Select a storage location and tap **Select**.

3 Enter contact information.

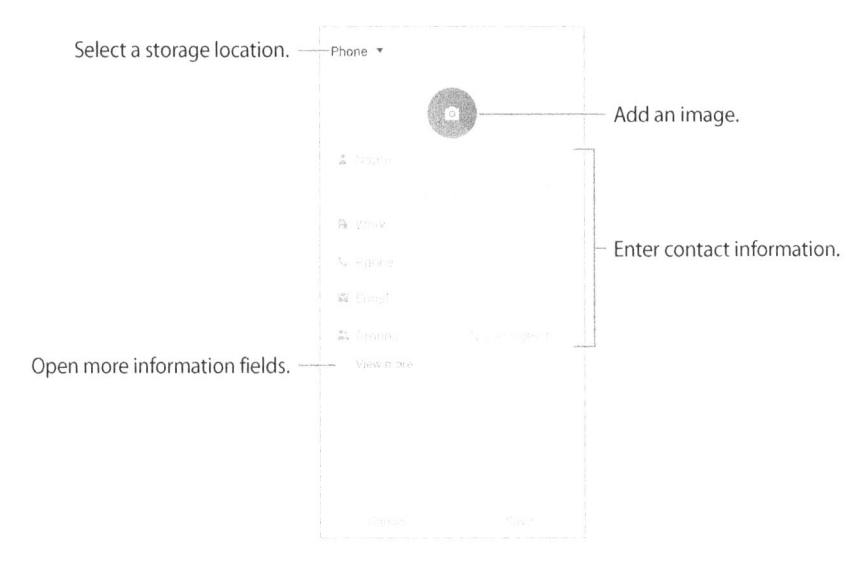

Select a storage location.

Add an image.

Enter contact information.

Open more information fields.

Depending on the selected storage location, the types of information you can save may vary.

4 Tap **Save**.

87

Apps and features

Importing contacts

Add contacts by importing them from other storages to your device.

1 Launch the **Contacts** app and tap ≡ → **Manage contacts** → **Import/Export contacts** → **Import**.

2 Select a storage location to import contacts from.

3 Tick VCF files or contacts to import and tap **Done**.

4 Select a storage location to save contacts to and tap **Import**.

Syncing contacts with your web accounts

Sync your device contacts with online contacts saved in your web accounts, such as your Samsung account.

1 Launch the **Settings** app, tap **Accounts and backup** → **Accounts** and select the account to sync with.

2 Tap **Sync account** and tap the **Contacts** switch to activate it.

For the Samsung account, tap ⋮ → **Sync settings** and tap the **Contacts** switch to activate it.

Searching for contacts

Launch the **Contacts** app.
Use one of the following search methods:

- Scroll up or down the contacts list.
- Drag a finger along the index at the right side of the contacts list to scroll through it quickly.
- Tap 🔍 at the top of the contacts list and enter search criteria.

Apps and features

Tap the contact. Then take one of the following actions:

- : Add to favourite contacts.
- / : Make a voice or video call.
- : Compose a message.
- : Compose an email.

Sharing contacts

You can share contacts with others by using various sharing options.

1 Launch the **Contacts** app and tap → **Share**.

2 Select contacts and tap **Share**.

3 Select a sharing method.

Saving and sharing profile

Save and share your profile information, such as your photo and status message, with others using the profile sharing feature.

- The profile sharing feature may not be available depending on the region or service provider.
- The profile sharing feature is only available for contacts who have activated the profile sharing feature on their device.

1 Launch the **Contacts** app and select your profile.

2 Tap **Edit**, edit your profile, and tap **Save**.

3 Tap **Tap here to share your profile** and tap the switch to activate it.

To use the profile sharing feature, your phone number must be verified. You can view your contacts' updated profile information in **Contacts**.

To change the scope of contacts to share your profile with, tap **Select what's shared**, select an item to share, and then select an option.

Apps and features

Creating groups

You can add groups, such as family or friends, and manage contacts by group.

1 Launch the **Contacts** app and tap ≡ → **Groups** → **Create group**.

2 Enter a group name.
   To set a group ringtone, tap **Group ringtone** and select a ringtone.

3 Tap **Add member**, select contacts to add to the group, and then tap **Done**.

4 Tap **Save**.

Sending a group message

You can send a group message to a group's members at the same time.
Launch the **Contacts** app, tap ≡ → **Groups**, select a group, and then tap ⋮ → **Send message**.

Merging duplicate contacts

When you import contacts from other storages, or sync contacts with other accounts, your contacts list may include duplicate contacts. Merge duplicate contacts into one to streamline your contacts list.

1 Launch the **Contacts** app and tap ≡ → **Manage contacts** → **Merge contacts**.

2 Tick contacts and tap **Merge**.

Deleting contacts

1 Launch the **Contacts** app and tap ⋮ → **Delete**.

2 Select contacts and tap **Delete**.

To delete contacts one by one, open the contacts list and tap a contact. Then tap ⋮ → **Delete**.

Apps and features

Messages

Introduction

Send and view messages by conversation.

Sending messages

> You may incur additional charges for sending messages when you are roaming.

1 Launch the **Messages** app and tap .

2 Add recipients and enter a message.

To record and send a voice message, tap and hold , say your message, and then release your finger. The recording icon appears only while the keyboard is hidden.

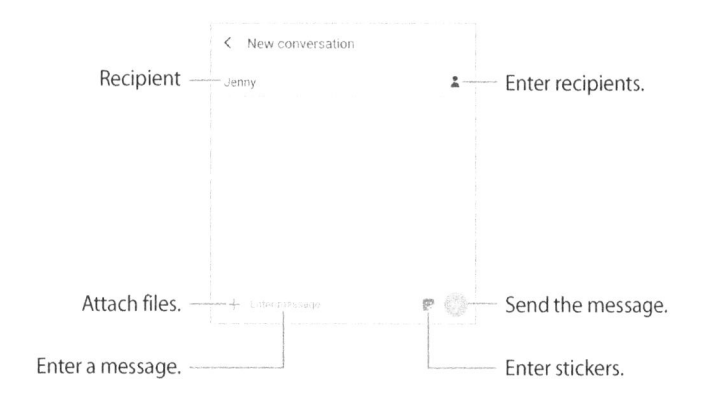

Recipient — Jenny
Enter recipients.
Attach files.
Send the message.
Enter a message.
Enter stickers.

3 Tap to send the message.

Apps and features

Sending My Emoji stickers

You can send My Emoji stickers that look like you via messages.

While composing a message, tap ![icon] and tap the My Emoji icon. My Emoji stickers will appear. Select the sticker that you want to share.

> My Emoji stickers will appear after you create My Emoji in the **Camera** app. Refer to Creating My Emoji for more information.

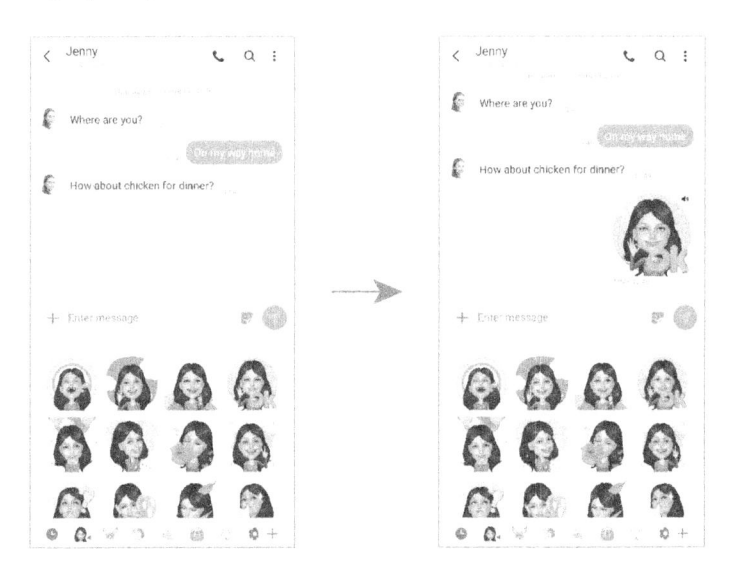

Apps and features

Viewing messages

Messages are grouped into message threads by contact.

You may incur additional charges for receiving messages when you are roaming.

1 Launch the **Messages** app and tap **Conversations**.

2 On the messages list, select a contact.

3 View your conversation.
To reply to the message, tap **Enter message**, enter a message, and then tap .
To adjust the font size, spread two fingers apart or pinch on the screen.

Blocking unwanted messages

Block messages from specific numbers added to your block list.

1 Launch the **Messages** app and tap → **Settings** → **Block numbers and messages** → **Block numbers**.

2 Tap **Inbox** and select a contact. Or, tap **Contacts**, select contacts, and then tap **Done**.
To manually enter a number, enter a phone number under **Enter number** and tap .

Apps and features

Setting the message notification

You can change notification sound, display options, and more.

1 Launch the **Messages** app, tap → **Settings** → **Notifications**, and then tap the switch to activate it.

2 Change the notification settings.

Setting a message reminder

You can set an alert at an interval to let you know that you have unchecked notifications. If this feature is not activated, launch the **Settings** app, tap **Accessibility** → **Advanced settings** → **Notification reminders**, and then tap the switch to activate it.

Deleting messages

1 Launch the **Messages** app and tap **Conversations**.

2 On the messages list, select a contact.

3 Tap and hold a message, tap **Delete**.

 To delete multiple messages, tick messages you want to delete.

4 Tap **Delete**.

Apps and features

Internet

Introduction

Browse the Internet to search for information and bookmark your favourite webpages to access them conveniently.

Browsing webpages

1 Open the **Samsung** folder and launch the **Internet** app.

2 Tap the address field.

3 Enter the web address or a keyword, and then tap **Go**.

To view the toolbars, drag your finger downwards slightly on the screen.

To switch between tabs quickly, swipe to the left or right on the address field.

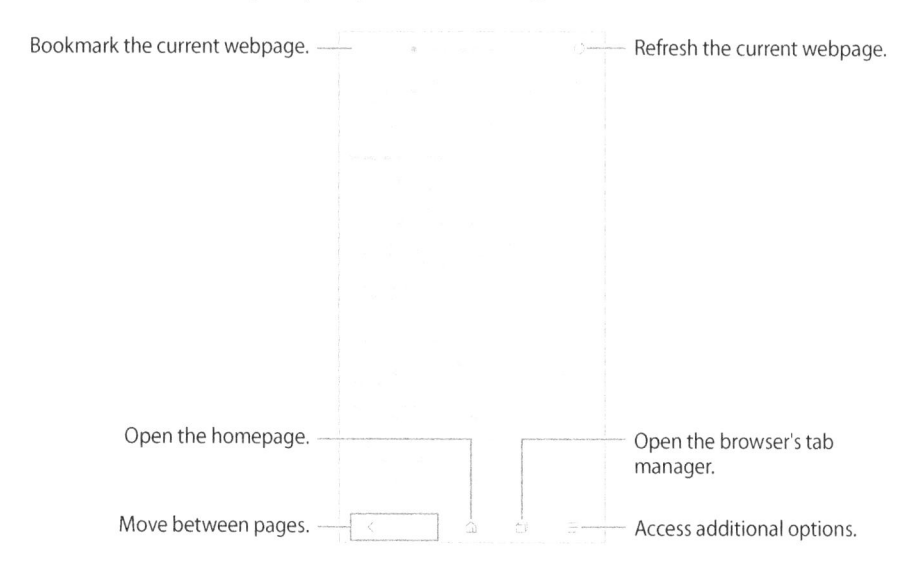

Bookmark the current webpage.
Refresh the current webpage.

Open the homepage.
Open the browser's tab manager.

Move between pages.
Access additional options.

Apps and features

Using secret mode

In secret mode, you can separately manage open tabs, bookmarks, and saved pages. You can lock secret mode using a password and your biometric data.

Activating secret mode

In the toolbar at the bottom of the screen, tap → **Turn on Secret mode**. If you are using this feature for the first time, set whether to use a password for secret mode.

In secret mode, the device will change the colour of the toolbars.

In secret mode, you cannot use some features, such as screen capture.

Changing security settings

You can change your password or the lock method.

Tap → **Settings** → **Privacy and security** → **Set Secret mode lock** → **Change password**. To set your registered biometric data as the lock method along with the password, tap the **Fingerprints**, **Irises**, or **Intelligent Scan** switch to activate it. Refer to Fingerprint recognition, Iris recognition, or Intelligent Scan for more information about using your biometric data.

Deactivating secret mode

In the toolbar at the bottom of the screen, tap → **Turn off Secret mode**.

Apps and features

Email

Setting up email accounts

Set up an email account when opening **Email** for the first time.

1 Open the **Samsung** folder and launch the **Email** app.

2 On the list, select an email service or tap **Other**.

3 Follow the on-screen instructions to complete the setup.

To set up another email account, tap ≡ → ✿ → **Add account**.

If you have more than one email account, you can set one as the default account. Tap ≡ → ✿ → ⋮ → **Set default account**.

Sending emails

1 Tap ✉ to compose an email.

2 Add recipients and enter a subject line and text.

3 Tap ➤ to send the mail.

Reading emails

When **Email** is open, the device will automatically retrieve new emails. To manually retrieve emails, swipe downwards on the top of the emails list.

Tap an email on the screen to read it.

If email syncing is disabled, new emails cannot be retrieved. To enable email syncing, tap ≡ → ✿ → your account name, and then tap the **Sync account** switch to activate it.

Apps and features

Camera

Introduction

Take photos and record videos using various modes and settings.

Camera etiquette

- Do not take photos or record videos of other people without their permission.
- Do not take photos or record videos where legally prohibited.
- Do not take photos or record videos in places where you may violate other people's privacy.

Launching Camera

Use the following methods to launch Camera:

- Launch the **Camera** app.
- Press the Power key twice quickly.
- On the locked screen, drag outside the circle.

- Some methods may not be available depending on the region or service provider.
- Some camera features are not available when you launch the **Camera** app from the locked screen or when the screen is turned off while the screen lock method is set.
- If photos you take appear blurry, clean the camera lens and try again.

Apps and features

Basic shooting

Taking photos or recording videos

1 On the shooting modes list, tap **Photo** or **Video**.

2 Tap the image on the preview screen where the camera should focus.

3 Tap ○ to take a photo or tap ⦿ to record a video.

- Options for current shooting mode
- AR Emoji
- Bixby Vison
- Camera settings
- Scene optimiser button
- Current mode
- Switch between the front and rear cameras.
- Take a photo.
- Preview thumbnail
- Shooting modes
- Select a lens (Galaxy S9+ models only).

- To adjust the brightness of photos or videos, tap the screen. When the adjustment bar appears, drag ☀ on the adjustment bar towards ➕ or ➖.
- To capture an image from the video while recording, tap ⧉.
- To change the focus while recording a video, tap where you want to focus. To use auto focus mode, tap ⓐ.

Apps and features

- The preview screen may vary depending on the shooting mode and which camera is being used.
- The camera automatically shuts off when unused.
- Make sure that the lens is not damaged or contaminated. Otherwise, the device may not work properly in some modes that require high resolutions.
- Your device's camera features a wide-angle lens. Minor distortion may occur in wide-angle photos or videos and does not indicate device performance problems.
- The maximum recording time may reduce when you record video at high resolution.

Selecting a lens for shooting (Galaxy S9+ models only)

Take a photo or record a video after selecting the camera lens you want.

On the preview screen, select a lens.

This feature is available only in some modes.

- ⓒ : You can take a basic photo or record a normal video with the normal lens.
- ⓞ : You can take a photo or record a video much clearer by enlarging the subject with the 2x optical zoom lens.

ⓒ Basic shooting   ⓞ 2x optical zoom shooting

Apps and features

Zooming in and out

Spread two fingers apart on the screen to zoom in, and pinch to zoom out.

- Zooming features are available only when using the rear camera.
- If you use the video zoom feature for a long time while recording a video, the video quality may diminish to prevent your device from overheating. (Galaxy S9+ models only)
- The 2x optical zoom may not work in low-light environments. (Galaxy S9+ models only)

Editing the shooting modes list

You can edit the shooting modes list on the preview screen.

1 On the preview screen, tap ⚙ → **Camera modes** → **Edit modes**.

Alternatively, tap and hold the shooting modes list on the preview screen.

2 Tick modes to use.

To change the order of shooting modes, drag ◇ to another location.

Shooting modes list

101

Apps and features

Setting the camera button action

You can take a series of photos or create an animated GIF by tapping and holding the camera button.

On the preview screen, tap ⚙ → **Hold Shutter button to** and select an action you want to use.

- **Take a picture**: Take a photo.
- **Take burst shot**: Take a series of photos.
- **Create GIF**: Create an animated GIF with sequential photos you taken.

 The **Take burst shot** and **Create GIF** features are available only in some shooting modes.

Using the focus and exposure features

Locking the focus (AF) and exposure (AE)

You can lock the focus or exposure on a selected area to prevent the camera from automatically adjusting based on changes to the subjects or light sources.

Tap and hold the area to focus, the AF/AE frame will appear on the area and the focus and exposure setting will be locked. The setting remains locked even after you take a photo.

 This feature is available only in **Photo** or **Pro** modes.

Apps and features

Separating the focus area and the exposure area

You can separate the focus area and the exposure area.

Tap and hold the preview screen. The AF/AE frame will appear on the screen. Drag the frame to the area where you want to separate the focus area and the exposure area.

This feature is available only in **Pro** mode.

Apps and features

Intelligent camera

Scene optimiser

Your device will adjust the colour settings automatically after recognising a subject or scene, such as people, food, or night scene.

On the shooting modes list, tap **Photo**. When the camera recognises the subject or scene, the scene optimiser button will change and the optimised colour will be applied.

Flaw detection

If a photo is taken poorly, the device will notify you to take the photo again.

When someone blinks or appears blurry in photos, or if there are smudges on the lens, a notification will appear after you take the photo.

If you do not want to use this feature, tap ⚙ on the preview screen and tap the **Flaw detection** switch to deactivate it.

Apps and features

Super Slow-mo

Super slow motion is a feature that records a quickly passing moment slowly so that you can appreciate it later. After the video is recorded, background music will be added automatically.

Some super slow motion features may differ depending on the model.

How to record in super slow motion

You can record super slow motion videos in the Single-take and Multi-take modes.

On the preview screen, tap ⚙ → **Super Slow-mo** and select a mode you want.

- **Multi-take**: Record a video and capture multiple moments in super slow motion.
- **Single-take**: Record a short video by capturing a single moment in super slow motion.

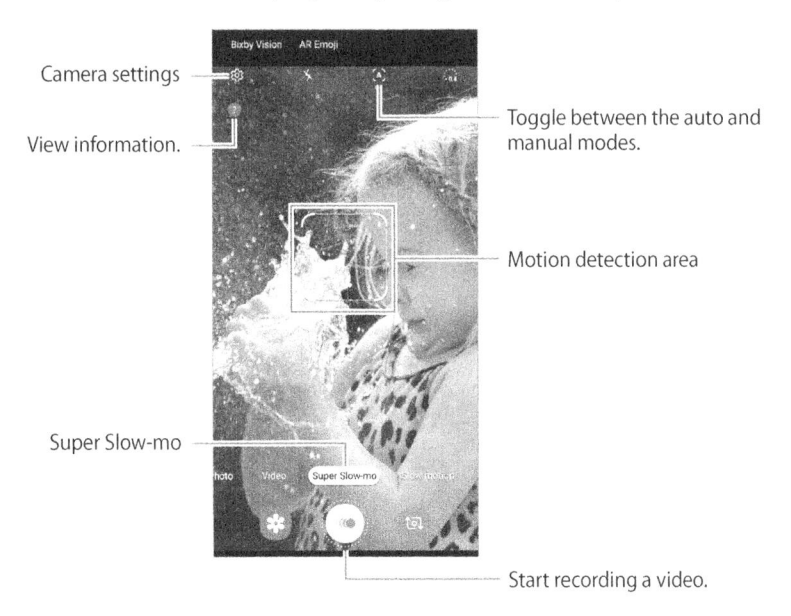

Camera settings

View information.

Toggle between the auto and manual modes.

Motion detection area

Super Slow-mo

Start recording a video.

Apps and features

- Use this feature in a place that has sufficient light. When recording a video indoors with insufficient or poor lighting, some of the following situations may occur:
  - The screen may appear dark due to the small amount of light.
  - The screen may flicker in certain lighting conditions, such as fluorescent light.
- Super slow motion recording may start at an unwanted moment if there are conditions such as the following:
  - When the device shakes.
  - When another object is moving near the subject in the motion detection area.
  - When recording under flickering light, such as a fluorescent light.
  - When recording in dark areas where noise occurs.

Recording super slow motion videos in single-take mode

Record a short video by capturing a single moment that the subject is moving.

1 On the shooting modes list, tap **Super Slow-mo**.

2 Select the mode you want.

- (Manual): You can capture the moment you want in super slow motion.
- (Auto): When motion is detected in the motion detection area, the device will capture the moment in super slow motion.

Apps and features

3 Tap .

The device will capture the moment in super slow motion and save it as a short video.

Manual single-shot   Auto single-shot

Recording super slow motion videos in multi-take mode

While recording a video, you can capture the moments that the subject is moving in super slow motion.

1 On the shooting modes list, tap **Super Slow-mo**.

2 On the preview screen, tap ⚙ → **Super Slow-mo** → **Multi-take** and double-tap the Back button.

Apps and features

3 Select the mode you want.
   - (M) (Manual): At the moment you want to capture in super slow motion, tap ⊙.
   - (A) (Auto): When motion is detected in the motion detection area, the device will capture the moment in super slow motion.

4 Tap ⊙ to start recording a video.
   You can use super slow motion up to 20 times in a single video.

5 Tap ▪ to stop recording the video.

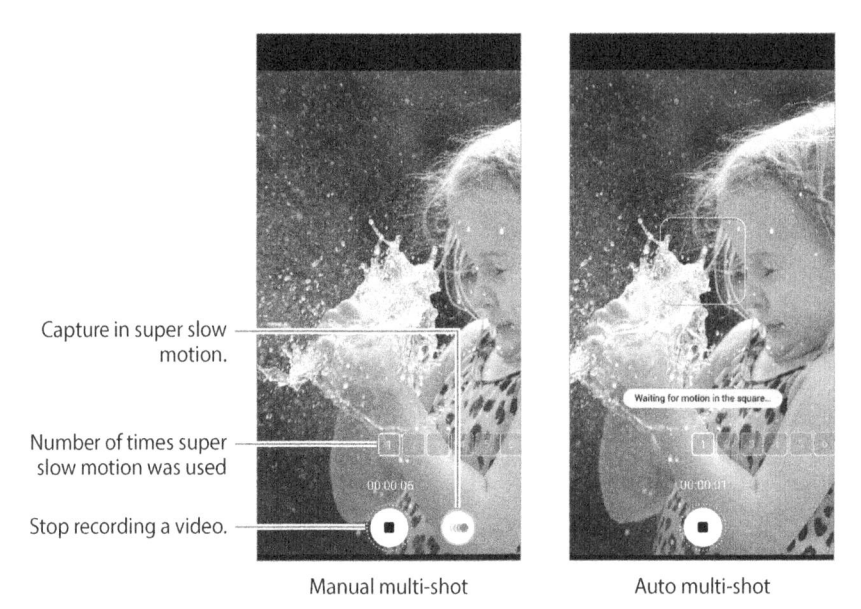

Capture in super slow motion.

Number of times super slow motion was used

Stop recording a video.

Manual multi-shot   Auto multi-shot

Changing the motion detection area

To move the motion detection area, tap the area inside the frame and drag it to a new location. To adjust the area size, tap a corner of the frame and drag it.

Apps and features

Playing super slow motion videos

Select a super slow motion video and tap **Super Slow-mo**.

Random background music will automatically accompany the video during playback.

To capture an image while playing a video, tap .

Editing super slow motion videos

On the playback screen, you can edit the video and save it as a different file or share it.

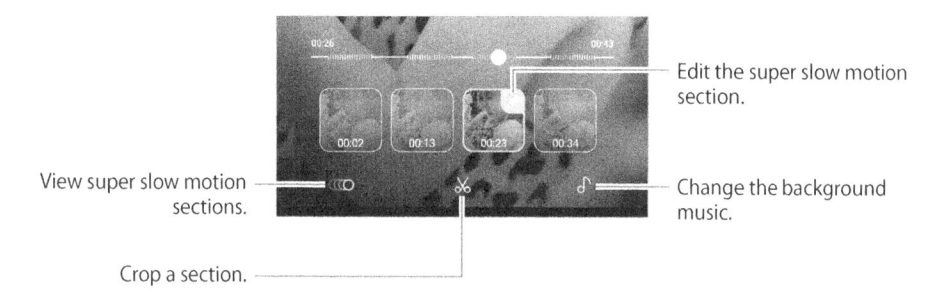

- Edit the super slow motion section.
- View super slow motion sections.
- Change the background music.
- Crop a section.

- : Select and view a super slow motion section of the video. If you want to turn off the super slow motion effect, tap and then tap the **Super slow** switch to deactivate it.
- : Crop out a desired section. Drag the start bracket and the end bracket to the desired points to select the section to keep.

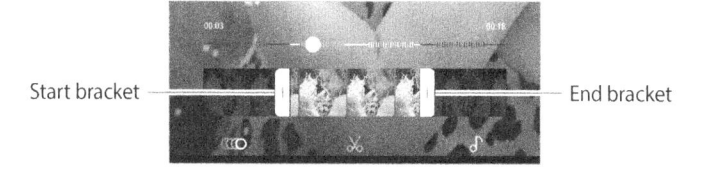

Start bracket — End bracket

- : Change the background music.

Apps and features

Sharing super slow motion clips

1 Select a super slow motion video and drag upwards on the video preview screen. Short clips with different effects will appear.

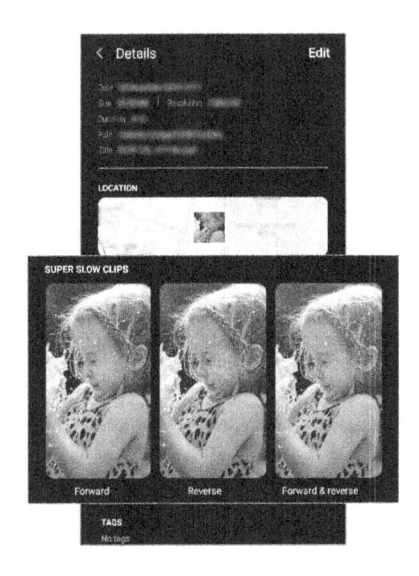

2 Select a clip you want and tap **Share**.

3 Select a file format and a sharing method.

- Some social network services and messenger apps may not support the sharing feature.
- This feature is only available for unedited original videos recorded in super slow motion.

Apps and features

Live focus (Galaxy S9+ models only)

The dual camera allows you to take shallow focus photos where the background is blurred and the subject stands out clearly. Moreover, the Dual capture feature allows you to take a close-up photo zoomed in on the subject and a wide angle photo with a broader background, all in one shot.

Taking portraits that stand out using the Live focus feature

Adjust the background blur level on the preview screen and take a photo that highlights the subject.

- Use this feature in a place that has sufficient light.
- The background blur may not be applied properly in the following conditions:
    - The device or the subject is moving.
    - The subject is thin or transparent.
    - The subject has a similar colour or pattern to the background.
    - The subject or background is plain.

1 On the shooting modes list, tap **Live focus**.

2 Drag the background blur adjustment bar to the left or right to adjust the blur level.

Apps and features

3 When **Live focus ready.** appears on the preview screen, tap ⬤ to take a photo.

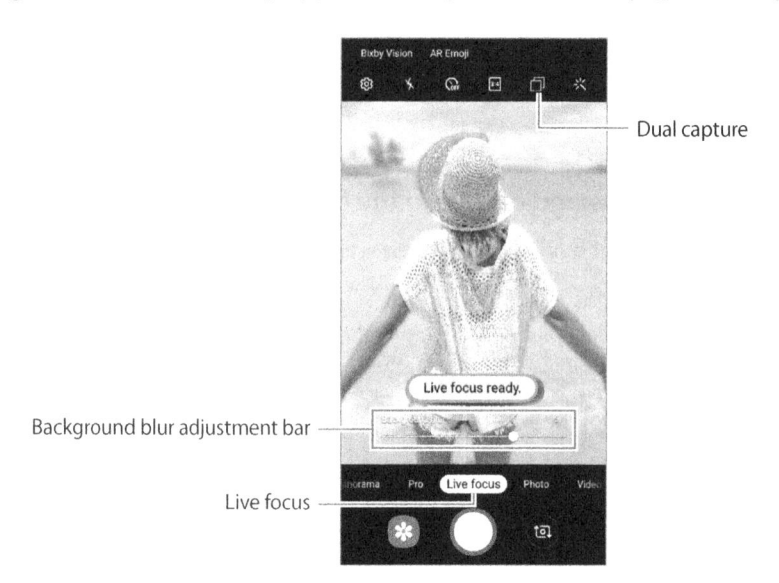

Dual capture

Background blur adjustment bar

Live focus

Apps and features

Editing the background of the Live Focus photos

You can also edit the background blur level of a photo taken with the Live focus feature. When the background lighting appears in blurred points, you can change the shape of the background blur. Select a shape, such as a heart, star, or flower, to decorate the photo and make it look different.

1 Select a photo taken with the Live focus feature and tap **Change background effect**.

2 To adjust the background blur level, drag the background blur adjustment bar to the left or right.

To change the background blur shape, drag the effect list to the left or right and select an effect you want. The effect list will appear only when the photo has blur shape in the background.

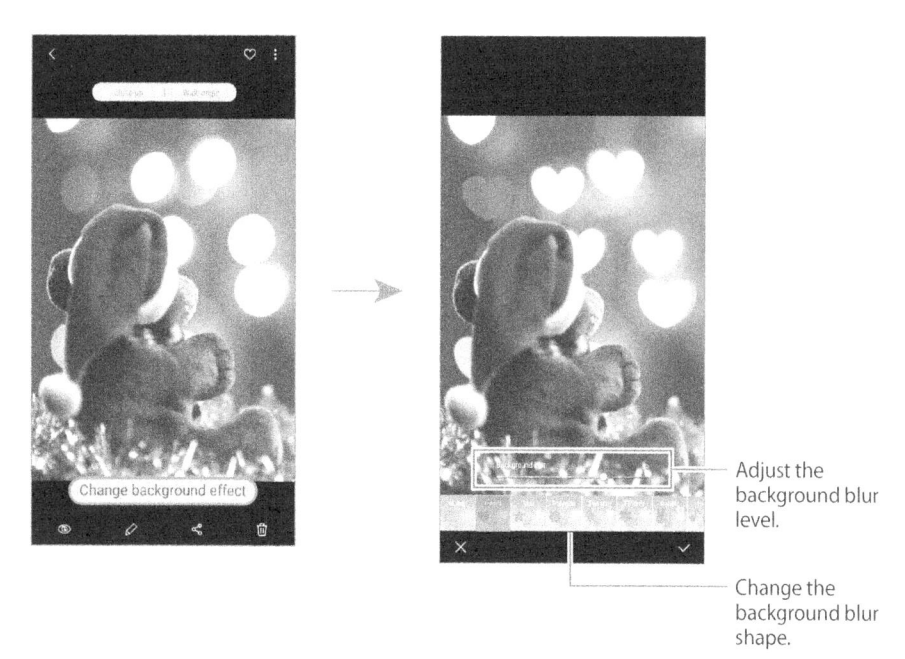

Adjust the background blur level.

Change the background blur shape.

3 Tap **Apply** to save the photo.

Apps and features

Taking the hidden background with the Dual capture feature

With one shot, you can capture both a close-up photo and a wide angle photo with a broader background. You can view the background scenery which was hidden on the preview screen.

On the shooting modes list, tap **Live focus**. Make sure the Dual capture feature is activated ( ), and then take a photo. Select the photo and view the close-up and wide angle photos.

A close-up photo   A wide angle photo

AR Emoji

Create a My Emoji that look just like you. You can now send stickers made with My Emoji to liven up any conversation.

You can take photos and record videos using AR Emojis, such as My Emoji or Live stickers, which mimic your expressions.

Apps and features

Creating My Emoji

Make a My Emoji that looks like you. My Emoji stickers with various expressions will be automatically generated.

1 On the preview screen, tap **AR Emoji** → **Create My Emoji**.

2 Align your face on the screen and tap ⭘ to take a photo.

3 Select My Emoji's gender and tap **Next**.

4 Decorate My Emoji.
 To edit details, such as the eye colour or face shape, tap ⚙.

5 Tap ✓.
 When a pop-up window appears, tick **Save My Emoji stickers in Gallery** and tap **OK**.

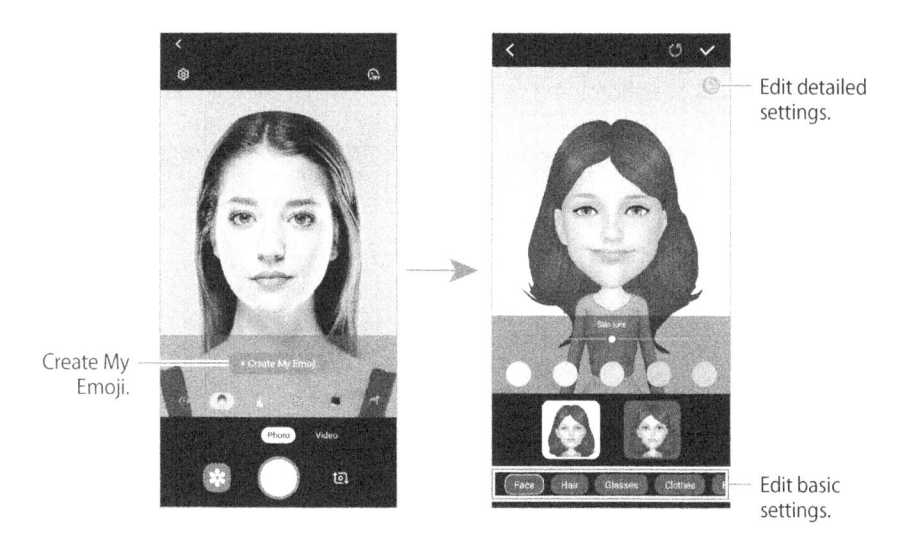

Create My Emoji.

Edit detailed settings.

Edit basic settings.

You can use the **AR Emoji** feature in both the front and rear cameras. If you are using the rear camera, it will automatically switch to the front camera. To switch between cameras, swipe upwards or downwards, or tap ⟲.

Apps and features

Deleting My Emoji

Tap and hold the My Emoji that you want to delete and tap —.

Taking fun photos with AR Emoji

Create a fun photo or video using an AR Emoji that mimics your expressions.

1 On the preview screen, tap **AR Emoji**.

2 Select an AR Emoji you want.

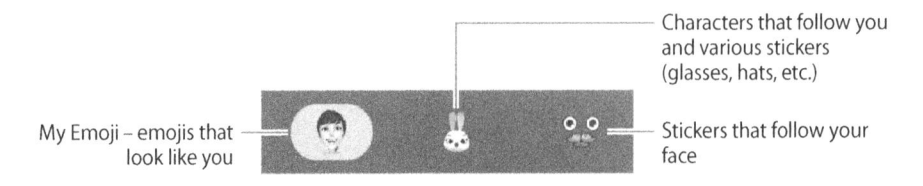

My Emoji – emojis that look like you

Characters that follow you and various stickers (glasses, hats, etc.)

Stickers that follow your face

3 Tap ◯ to take a photo or tap **Video** → ⦿ to record a video.

You can check out photos and videos that you have recorded in **Gallery** and share them.

116

Apps and features

Applying stickers randomly

You can apply stickers randomly, instead of selecting one from the stickers list.

Tap **Random** repeatedly until the sticker you want appears.

Enjoying My Emoji stickers while chatting

You can use My Emoji stickers during a conversation via messages or on a social network.

1 On the Samsung keyboard, tap .

2 Tap the My Emoji icon.

3 Select one of the My Emoji stickers.

   The My Emoji sticker will be inserted.

My Emoji icon

Deleting My Emoji stickers

On the Samsung keyboard, tap and tap at the bottom of the keyboard. Select the My Emoji stickers you want to delete and tap **Delete**.

Apps and features

Using shooting modes

To change the shooting mode, drag the shooting modes list to the left or right, or swipe to the left or right on the preview screen.

Select a shooting mode you want.

Photo mode

The camera adjusts the shooting options automatically based on the surroundings to capture photos easily.

On the shooting modes list, tap **Photo**.

To take self-portraits with the front camera, swipe upwards or downwards, or tap to switch to the front camera.

Applying beauty effects

You can select a filter effect and also modify your facial features, such as your skin tone or face shape, before taking a self-portrait.

1 On the preview screen, tap .

2 Select a filter effect or beauty effects and take a photo.

Video mode

The camera adjusts the shooting options automatically based on the surroundings to record videos easily.

On the shooting modes list, tap **Video**.

Apps and features

Pro mode

Capture photos while manually adjusting various shooting options, such as exposure value and ISO value.

On the shooting modes list, tap **Pro**. Select options and customise the settings, and then tap to take a photo.

Available options

- : Select an ISO value. This controls camera light sensitivity. Low values are for stationary or brightly lit objects. Higher values are for fast-moving or poorly lit objects. However, higher ISO settings can result in noise in photos.

    If the shutter speed is set manually, you cannot set the ISO setting to **AUTO**.

- : Adjust the shutter speed. A slow shutter speed allows more light in, so the photo becomes brighter. This is ideal for photos of scenery or photos taken at night. A fast shutter speed allows less light in. This is ideal for taking photos of fast-moving subjects. You can select an aperture value that will determine the brightness and depth of field. Tap **F1.5** or **F2.4**.

- : Adjust the colour tone.

- : Change the focus mode. Drag the adjustment bar towards or to manually adjust the focus. To switch to auto focus mode, tap **MANUAL**.

- : Select an appropriate white balance, so images have a true-to-life colour range. You can set the colour temperature.

- : Change the exposure value. This determines how much light the camera's sensor receives. For low-light situations, use a higher exposure.

    If the shutter speed is set manually, you cannot change the exposure value. The exposure value will change and be displayed based on the shutter speed setting.

Apps and features

Food mode

Take photos of food with more vibrant colours.

1 On the shooting modes list, tap **Food**.

2 Tap the screen and drag the circular frame over the area to highlight.
The area outside the circular frame will be blurred.
To resize the circular frame, drag a corner of the frame.

3 Tap ⊛ and drag the adjustment bar to adjust the colour tone.

4 Tap ○ to take a photo.

Apps and features

Panorama mode

Using panorama mode, take a series of photos and then stitch them together to create a wide scene.

> To get the best shots using panorama mode, follow these tips:
> - Move the camera slowly in one direction.
> - Keep the image within the frame on the camera's viewfinder. If the preview image is out of the guide frame or you do not move the device, the device will automatically stop taking photos.
> - Avoid taking photos of indistinct backgrounds, such as an empty sky or a plain wall.

1 On the shooting modes list, tap **Panorama**.

2 Tap ○ and move the device slowly in one direction.

3 Tap ● to stop taking photos.

Selective focus mode (Galaxy S9 models only)

Use the out-of-focus effect to make specific objects stand out in a photo.

1 On the shooting modes list, tap **Selective focus**.

2 Tap the image on the preview screen where the camera should focus.

3 Tap ○ to take a photo.

4 On the preview screen, tap the preview thumbnail.

Apps and features

5 Tap **Adjust background blur** and select one of the following:

- **Near focus**: Make the subject stand out and blur the background around the subject.
- **Far focus**: Blur the subject and make the background stand out around the subject.
- **Pan focus**: Make the subject and its background stand out.

6 Tap **SAVE**.

- It is recommended that you position subjects within 50 cm of the device. Position the subject that you want to focus on close to the device.
- When taking photos, ensure there is sufficient distance between the subject and the background. The distance should be more than three times the distance between the device and the subject.
- Hold the device steady and remain still while taking a photo.
- The quality of photos taken by the device can be affected in the following conditions:
  - The device or the subject is moving.
  - There is strong background light, low levels of light, or you are taking photos indoors.
  - The subject has a similar colour or pattern to the background.

Slow motion mode

Record a video for viewing it in slow motion. You can specify sections of your videos to be played in slow motion.

1 On the shooting modes list, tap **Slow motion**.

2 Tap ● to start recording.

3 When you are finished recording, tap ▪ to stop.

4 On the preview screen, tap the preview thumbnail.

122

Apps and features

5 Tap **Slow motion**.

The fastest section of the video will be set as a slow motion section and the video will start playing. Up to two slow motion sections will be created based on the video.

To edit the slow motion section, drag ● to the left or right.

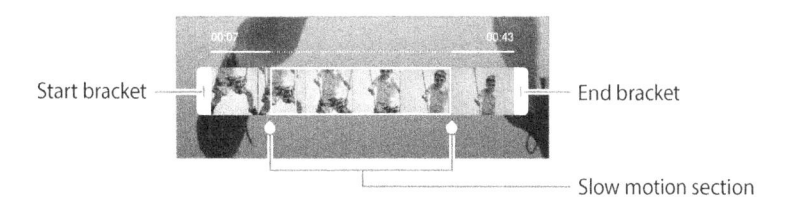

Start bracket — End bracket

Slow motion section

Hyperlapse mode

Record scenes, such as passing people or cars, and view them as fast-motion videos.

1 On the shooting modes list, tap **Hyperlapse**.

2 Tap ⓖ and select a frame rate option.

If you set the frame rate to **Auto**, the device will automatically adjust the frame rate according to the changing rate of the scene.

3 Tap ● to start recording.

4 Tap ■ to finish recording.

5 On the preview screen, tap the preview thumbnail and tap **Hyperlapse** to view the video.

Sports mode

Take clearer photos of fast-moving subjects, such as a person running or a pet in motion.

On the shooting modes list, tap **Sports**.

You must first add this mode to the shooting modes list before you can use it. On the preview screen, tap ⚙ → **Camera modes** → **Edit modes**, and then tick **Sports**.

Apps and features

Wide selfie mode

Take a wide self-portrait and include as many people in the photo as possible to avoid leaving people out.

> You must first add this mode to the shooting modes list before you can use it. On the preview screen, tap ⚙ → **Camera modes** → **Edit modes**, and then tick **Wide selfie**.

1 On the preview screen, swipe upwards or downwards, or tap 📷 to switch to the front camera for self-portraits.

2 On the shooting modes list, tap **Wide selfie**.

3 Face the front camera lens.

4 Tap ○ to take a photo.

Alternatively, show your palm to the front camera. After recognising your palm, a countdown timer will appear. When the time is up, the device will take a photo.

5 Slowly swivel the device left and then right or vice versa to take a wide self-portrait.

The device will take additional photos when the white frame moves to each end of the viewfinder window.

> - Make sure to keep the white frame inside the viewfinder window.
> - The subjects should remain still while taking wide self-portraits.
> - The top and bottom parts of the image displayed on the preview screen may be cut out of the photo depending on the shooting conditions.

Apps and features

Customising camera settings

Options for current shooting mode

On the preview screen, use the following options.

The available options may vary depending on the shooting mode.

- : Activate or deactivate the flash.
- : Select the length of the delay before the camera automatically takes a photo.
- : Apply beauty effects or a filter effect.
- : Select a frame rate.
- / : Select an aspect ratio for videos.
- : Select a metering method. This determines how light values are calculated. **Centre-weighted** uses the light in the centre portion of the shot to calculate the exposure of the shot. [o] **Spot** uses the light in a concentrated centre area of the shot to calculate the exposure of the shot. **Matrix** averages the entire scene.
- : Change the focus area in auto focus mode. **Multi AF** focuses on several areas within the frame. Multiple rectangles will appear to indicate the focused areas. **Centre AF** focuses on the centre within the frame.
- : In **Food** mode, focus on a subject inside the circular frame and blur the image outside the frame.
- : In **Food** mode, adjust the colour tone.
- : Activate or deactivate the Dual capture feature. (Galaxy S9+ models only)
- : Toggle between the auto and manual modes when recording super slow-mo videos.
- : Change the recording time of super slow-mo videos.

125

Apps and features

Camera settings

On the preview screen, tap ⚙. Some options may not be available depending on the shooting mode.

Intelligent features

- **Scene optimiser**: Set the device to adjust the colour settings automatically depending on the subject or scene.
- **Flaw detection**: Set to receive notifications when someone blinks or appears blurry in photos, or if there are smudges on the lens.

Pictures

- **Rear picture size**: Select a resolution for photos you want to take with the rear camera. Using a higher resolution will result in higher quality photos, but they will take up more memory.
- **Front picture size**: Select a resolution for photos you want to take with the front camera. Using a higher resolution will result in higher quality photos, but they will take up more memory.
- **Motion photos**: Set the device to take a video clip for a few seconds before tapping ◯. This allows you to capture a moment you might have missed. To view the video, tap the preview thumbnail and tap **View motion photo**. To capture a still image from the video clip, tap the screen to stop playback and tap **Capture**. This feature is available only in **Photo** mode.
- **Hold Shutter button to**: Select an action to perform when you tap and hold the camera button.
- **Save options**: Select how you want to save photos.

   Tap the **RAW copies (Pro)** switch to set the device to save photos as uncompressed RAW files (DNG file format) in pro mode. RAW files retain all of a photo's data for the best image quality, but they will take up more memory.

   > When using the **RAW copies (Pro)** feature, each photo is saved in two formats, DNG and JPG.

Apps and features

Videos

- **Rear video size**: Select a resolution for videos you want to take with the rear camera. Using a higher resolution will result in higher quality videos, but they will take up more memory.

    If you activate the **High efficiency video** feature, you can record videos in the High Efficiency Video Codec (HEVC) format. Your HEVC videos will be saved as compressed files to conserve the device's memory.

    - You cannot play the HEVC videos on other devices or share them online.
    - Super slow motion and slow motion videos cannot be recorded in the HEVC format.

- **Front video size**: Select a resolution for videos you want to take with the front camera. Using a higher resolution will result in higher quality videos, but they will take up more memory.

    If you activate the **High efficiency video** feature, you can record videos in the High Efficiency Video Codec (HEVC) format. Your HEVC videos will be saved as compressed files to conserve the device's memory.

    You cannot play the HEVC videos on other devices or share them online.

- **Super Slow-mo**: Select how you want to record super slow motion videos.
- **Video stabilisation**: Activate anti-shake to reduce or eliminate blurry image resulting from camera shake while recording a video.

    When the **Tracking auto-focus** feature is activated, you cannot use this feature.

Apps and features

Useful features

- **HDR (rich tone)**: Take photos with rich colours and reproduce details even in bright and dark areas.
- **Tracking auto-focus**: Set the device to track and automatically focus on a selected subject. When you select a subject on the preview screen, the device will focus on the subject even if the subject is moving or you change the camera's position.
    - When this feature is activated, you cannot use the Video stabilisation feature.
    - Tracking a subject may fail in the following conditions:
        - The subject is too big or too small.
        - The subject moves excessively.
        - The subject is backlit or you are shooting in a dark place.
        - Colours or patterns on the subject and the background are the same.
        - The subject includes horizontal patterns, such as blinds.
        - The camera shakes excessively.
        - The video resolution is high.
        - When zooming in or out using the 2x optical zoom. (Galaxy S9+ models only)
- **Grid lines**: Display viewfinder guides to help composition when selecting subjects.
- **Location tags**: Attach a GPS location tag to the photo.
    - GPS signal strength may decrease in locations where the signal is obstructed, such as between buildings or in low-lying areas, or in poor weather conditions.
    - Your location may appear on your photos when you upload them to the Internet. To avoid this, deactivate the location tag setting.
- **Selfie shape correction**: When your face is at the edges of the preview screen, it will appear distorted. Enable this option to correct your face shape. After shape correction, the background may appear slightly distorted.

Apps and features

- **Camera modes**: View available shooting modes or edit the shooting modes list.
- **Shooting methods**: Select a shooting method for taking a photo or recording a video.
- **Storage location**: Select the memory location for storage. This feature will appear when you insert a memory card.
- **Quick launch**: Set the device to launch the camera by pressing the Power key twice quickly.

This feature may not be available depending on the region or service provider.

- **Quick review**: Set the device to show photos after capturing them.
- **Reset settings**: Reset the camera settings.
- **Contact us**: Ask questions or view frequently asked questions. Refer to Samsung Members for more information.
- **About Camera**: View the Camera app version and legal information.

Gallery

Introduction

View images and videos stored in your device. You can also manage images and videos by album or create stories.

Viewing images

1 Launch the **Gallery** app and tap **Pictures**.

Apps and features

2 Select an image.

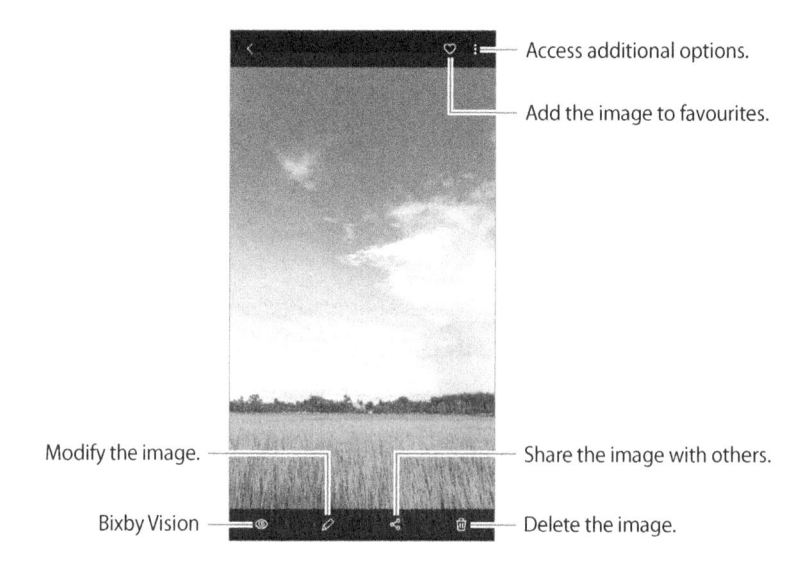

- Access additional options.
- Add the image to favourites.
- Modify the image.
- Share the image with others.
- Bixby Vision
- Delete the image.

You can create a movie, animated GIF, or collage from multiple images. On the list, tap ⋮ → **Create movie**, **Create GIF**, or **Create collage**, and then select images.

Searching for images

Launch the **Gallery** app and tap ○ to view images sorted by category, such as types, locations, or documents.

To search for images by entering keywords, tap the search field.

Editing the background of Live focus photos (Galaxy S9+ models only)

You can edit the background blur level of a photo taken with the Live Focus feature. If the background lighting of Live focus photos appears in blurred points, you can change the shape of the background blur.

Launch the **Gallery** app, select a photo taken with the Live focus feature, tap **Change background effect** to edit the blur level or change the shape of the background blur.

Apps and features

Viewing photos taken with the Dual capture feature (Galaxy S9+ models only)

View the close-up photo and the wide angle photo taken with the Dual capture feature.

Launch the **Gallery** app, select a photo taken with the Dual capture feature, and then tap **Close-up** or **Wide angle**.

Viewing videos

1 Launch the **Gallery** app and tap **Pictures**.

2 Select a video to play.

3 Tap **Video** to play the video.

- Rewind or fast-forward by dragging the bar.
- Capture the current screen.
- Switch to the pop-up video player.
- Lock the playback screen.
- Skip to the previous video. Tap and hold to rewind.
- Access additional options.
- Create an animated GIF.
- Change screen ratio.
- Rotate the screen
- Skip to the next video. Tap and hold to fast-forward.
- Pause and resume playback.

Drag your finger up or down on the left side of the playback screen to adjust the brightness, or drag your finger up or down on the right side of the playback screen to adjust the volume.

To rewind or fast-forward, swipe to the left or right on the playback screen.

Apps and features

Using the Video enhancer feature

Enhance the image quality of your videos to enjoy brighter and more vivid colours. Launch the **Settings** app, tap **Advanced features**, and then tap the **Video enhancer** switch to activate it.

- This feature is only available in some apps.
- Using this feature will increase battery consumption.

Viewing the details of images and videos

You can view file details, such as people, location, and basic information. If there is auto created content, such as a story or a GIF, the content will also be displayed.

While viewing an image or on the video preview screen, drag upwards on the screen. File details will appear.

You can also view related content by tapping information on the screen.

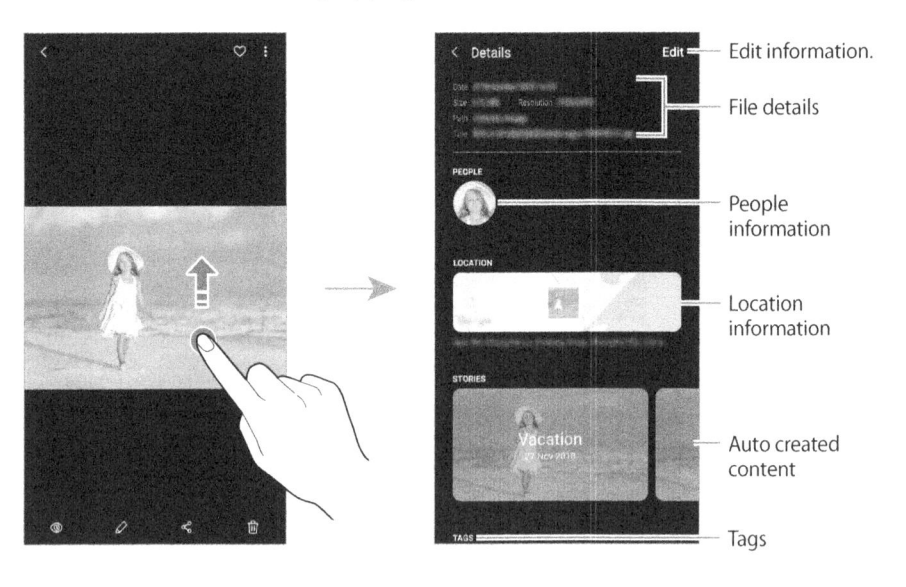

- Edit information.
- File details
- People information
- Location information
- Auto created content
- Tags

Apps and features

Viewing albums

You can view your images and videos sorted by folders or albums. The movies, animated GIFs, or collages that you have created will also be sorted in your folders on the albums list.

Launch the **Gallery** app, tap **Albums**, and then select an album.

Hiding albums

You can hide albums.

> You cannot hide albums created by default, such as the **Camera** and **Screenshots** albums.

1 Launch the **Gallery** app and tap **Albums**.

2 Tap **⋮** → **Hide or unhide albums**.

3 Tap an album switch to hide.

Viewing stories

When you capture or save images and videos, the device will read their date and location tags, sort the images and videos, and then create stories. To create stories automatically, you must capture or save multiple images and videos.

Launch the **Gallery** app, tap **Stories**, and then select a story.

Creating stories

Create stories with various themes.

1 Launch the **Gallery** app and tap **Stories**.

2 Tap **⋮** → **Create story**.

3 Enter a title for the story and tap **Create**.

4 Tick images or videos to include in the story and tap **Done**.

Apps and features

To add images or videos to a story, select a story and tap → **Add**.

To remove images or videos from a story, select a story, tap → **Edit**, tick images or videos to remove, and then tap **Remove from story**.

Deleting stories

1 Launch the **Gallery** app and tap **Stories**.

2 Tap and hold a story to delete, and tap **Delete**.

Sharing albums

Create albums and share them with your family and friends saved in your contacts. They can view shared albums on devices signed in to their Samsung account, such as smartphones, TVs, or refrigerators.

- To use this feature, your phone number must be verified.
- To use this feature, you must register and sign in to your Samsung account.
- You may incur additional charges when sharing files via the mobile network.

Creating albums to share

1 Launch the **Gallery** app and tap **Shared**.

2 Tap **Create shared album**.

When using this feature for the first time, you must first agree to the terms and conditions of Samsung Social.

3 Enter a title for the album and tap **Create**.

4 Select a group to share with.

5 Tap **OK**.

The recipients will receive a notification.

Apps and features

Adding images or videos to an album

1 Launch the **Gallery** app and tap **Shared**.

2 Select an album to add images or videos.

3 Tap ➕ and tick images or videos to add.

4 Tap **Done**.

Syncing images and videos with Samsung Cloud

When you sync your **Gallery** app with Samsung Cloud, photos and videos you take will also be saved in Samsung Cloud. You can view images and videos saved in Samsung Cloud in your **Gallery** app and from other devices.

Launch the **Gallery** app, tap ⋮ → **Settings**, and then tap the **Sync with Samsung Cloud** switch to activate it. The **Gallery** app and Samsung Cloud will be synced.

Deleting images or videos

Deleting an image or a video

Select an image or a video and tap 🗑 at the bottom of the screen.

Deleting multiple images and videos

1 On the Gallery screen, tap and hold an image or a video to delete.

2 Tick the images or videos to delete.

3 Tap **Delete**.

135

Apps and features

Always On Display

You can view information, such as the clock or calendar, or control music playback on the screen when it is turned off.

You can also check notifications for new messages or missed calls.

- The brightness of the Always On Display may change automatically depending on the lighting conditions.
- If the sensor at the top of the device is covered for a certain period, the Always On Display will turn off.

Setting how to display the Always On Display

You can select how to display the Always On Display. The Always On Display can be set to appear continuously or only appear when tapping the screen while it is turned off. Also, you can set the time to display the Always On Display.

Launch the **Settings** app, tap **Lock screen** → **Always On Display** → **Display mode**, and then select a mode you want.

Apps and features

Opening notifications on the Always On Display

When you receive message, missed call, or app notifications, notification icons will appear on the Always On Display. Double-tap a notification icon to view its notification.

If the screen is locked, you must unlock it to view notifications.

Controlling music playback on the Always On Display

You can control music playback on the Always On Display.

1 Launch the **Settings** app, tap **Lock screen** → **FaceWidgets**, and then tap the **Music Controller** switch to activate it.

2 To control music playback on the Always On Display, double-tap the clock.

3 Swipe to the left or right on the clock to move to the music controller.

4 Tap the icons to control the playback.

Apps and features

Displaying an image to the Always On Display

You can display an image on the Always On Display. You can also display an animated GIF.

1 Launch the **Settings** app → **Lock screen** → **Clock style** → **Always On Display**.

2 Drag the types list to the left and select the type with an image on it.

3 Tap and select an image.
   To insert an animated GIF, tap **GIF** and select a file.

4 Tap **Done**.

Deactivating the Always On Display feature

Launch the **Settings** app, tap **Lock screen**, and then tap the **Always On Display** switch to deactivate it.

Apps and features

Edge screen

Introduction

You can quickly access your favourite apps and features from the Edge panels.

Using the Edge panels

Drag the Edge panel handle towards the centre of the screen.

If the Edge panel handle is not visible, launch the **Settings** app, tap **Display** → **Edge screen**, and then tap the **Edge panels** switch to activate it.

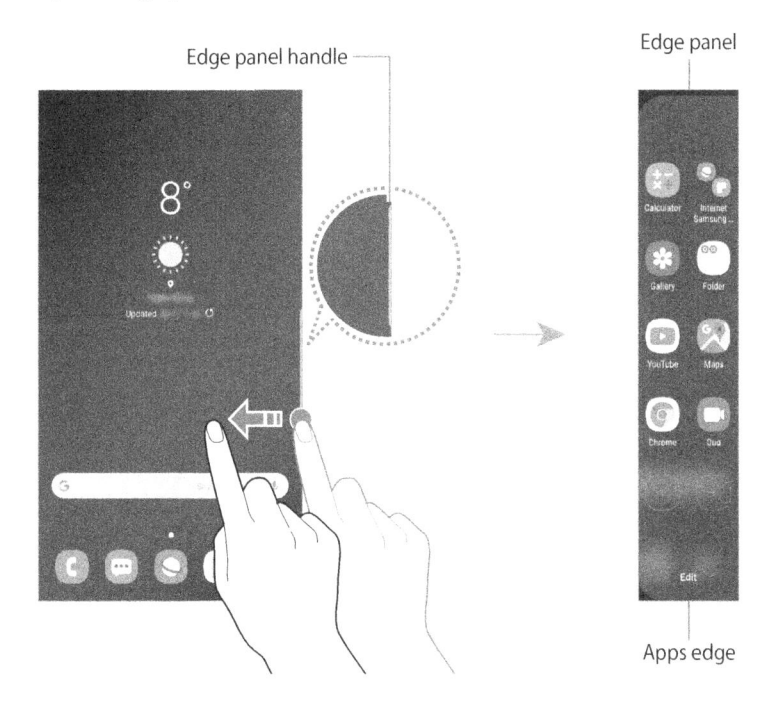

Edge panel handle

Edge panel

Apps edge

Apps and features

Editing the Edge panels

Select panels to display on the Edge screen or edit them.

1 Drag the Edge panel handle towards the centre of the screen.

2 Tap ✿ to open the Edge panel settings screen.

3 Tick Edge panels to display.
To edit a panel, tap **Edit**.
To download additional panels, tap ⋮ → **Galaxy Apps**.
To rearrange the panels, tap ⋮ → **Reorder** and drag ⟨ ⟩ to another location.

Setting the Edge panel handle

You can change the location, size, transparency, or vibration settings of the handle.

Drag the Edge panel handle towards the centre of the screen. Then, tap ✿ → ⋮ → **Edge panel handle**.

Apps edge

Quickly launch frequently used apps.

1 Drag the Edge panel handle towards the centre of the screen.

2 On the Apps edge panel, select an app to launch it.

Editing the Apps edge panel

- To add an app, tap ⊕ on the panel and tap an app from the apps list.
- To create a folder on the panel, tap ⊕ on the panel, tap and hold an app from the apps list, and then drag it over another app on the Apps edge panel. Drop the app when a folder frame appears around the apps.
- To delete an app, tap and hold an app on the panel and drag it to **Remove** at the top of the panel.
- To change the order of apps, tap and hold an app and drag it to another location.

You can also edit the Apps edge panel by tapping **Edit**.

Apps and features

Adding app pairs

Add two frequently used apps, such as a video player and a messenger app, to the Apps edge panel to launch them together in the split screen view with a single tap. For more information about the split screen view, refer to Split screen view.

1 Drag the Edge panel handle towards the centre of the screen.

2 On the Apps edge panel, tap (+) → **Create App pair**.

3 Select two apps from the list.

The first app will appear at the top and the second app will appear at the bottom when opened in the split screen view.

4 Tap **Done**.

Edge lighting

You can set the device to light up the edges of the screen and display a pop-up window when you receive notifications, such as new messages.

Even while the device's screen is facing downwards, the edges of the screen will light up to notify you of a call or new notifications. When a pop-up window appears while using an app, drag the window downwards to quickly view the content and perform available actions.

Managing notifications to display as the edge lighting

1 Launch the **Settings** app and tap **Display** → **Edge screen** → **Edge lighting**.

2 Tap **Manage notifications** and tap the switches next to apps to receive notifications as the edge lighting.

Some notifications may not display as the edge lighting depending on notification types.

Apps and features

Viewing notifications via the pop-up window

When you receive a notification with edge lighting, you can quickly view its content and perform available actions by opening the pop-up window. For example, if you receive a message while watching a video or playing a game, you can view the message and reply to it without switching the screen.

When you receive a notification with edge lighting while using an app, drag the notification downwards.

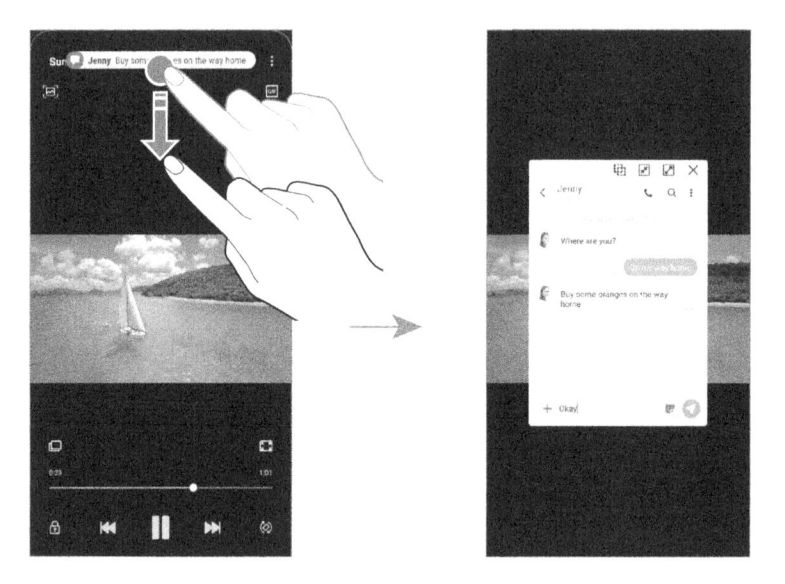

This feature is only available to apps that support the Multi window and edge lighting features. To view supported apps, launch the **Settings** app, tap **Display** → **Edge screen** → **Edge lighting** → **Manage notifications**.

Apps and features

Multi window

Introduction

Multi window lets you run two apps at the same time in the split screen view. You can also run multiple apps at the same time in the pop-up view.

Some apps may not support this feature.

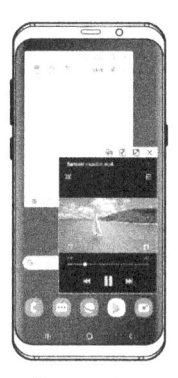

Split screen viewPop-up view

Split screen view

1 Tap the Recents button to open the list of recently used apps.

2 Swipe to the left or right, tap an app's icon, and then tap **Open in split screen view**.

The selected app will launch in the upper window.

Apps and features

3 On the lower window, swipe left or right to select another app to launch.

To launch apps not on the list of recently used apps, tap the Home button or Back button and select an app.

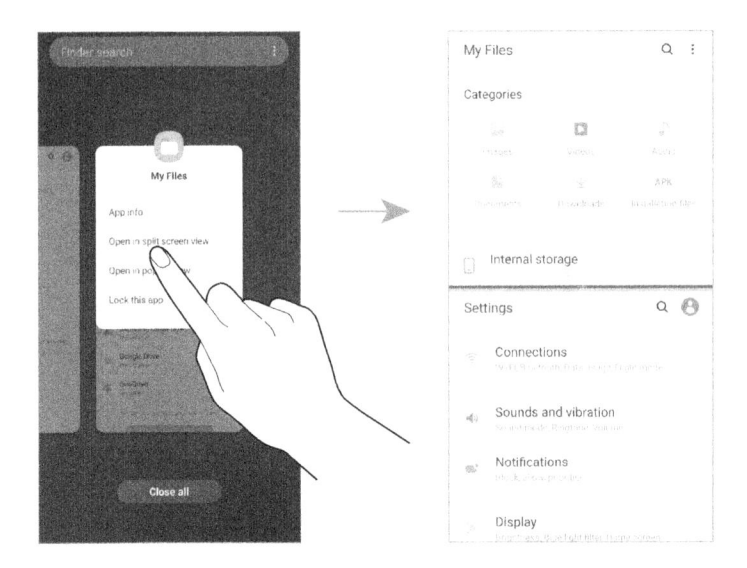

Adjusting the window size

Drag the bar between the app windows up or down to adjust the size of the windows.

When you drag the bar between the app windows to the top or bottom edge of the screen, the window will be maximised.

Apps and features

Pop-up view

1 Tap the Recents button to open the list of recently used apps.

2 Swipe to the left or right, tap an app's icon, and then tap **Open in pop-up view**.
The app screen will appear in the pop-up view.

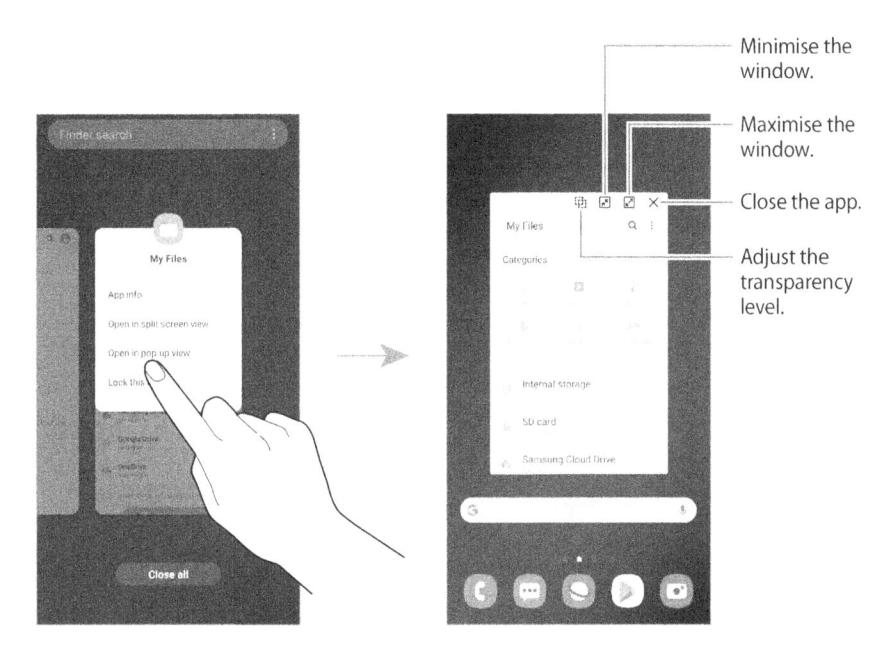

Minimise the window.

Maximise the window.

Close the app.

Adjust the transparency level.

Moving pop-up windows

To move a pop-up window, tap the window's toolbar and drag it to a new location.

Apps and features

Kids Home

Introduction

You can restrict children's access to certain apps, set their usage times, and configure settings to provide a fun and safe environment for children when they use the device.

Starting Kids Home

When starting Kids Home for the first time or after performing a data reset, follow the on-screen instructions to complete the setup.

1 Open the notification panel, swipe downwards on the notification panel, and then tap (**Kids Home**) to activate it.

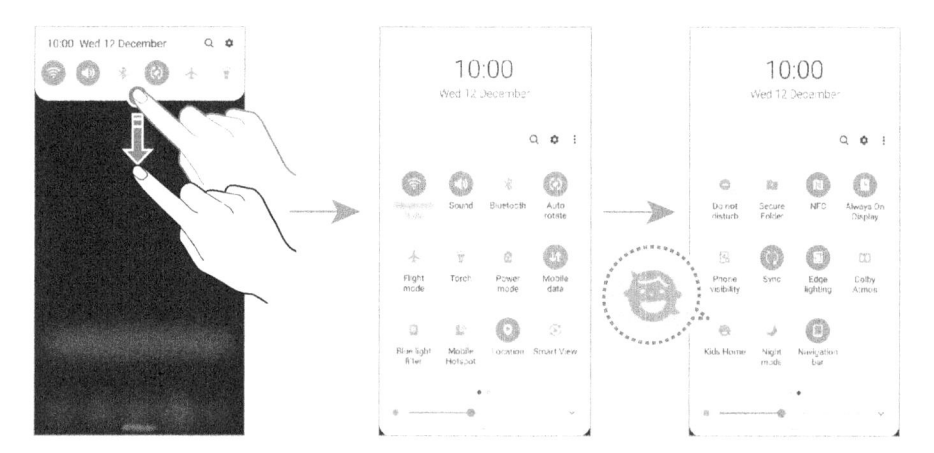

2 Tap **Start** to install Kids Home.

3 Read the Kids Home intro page and tap **Next**.

Apps and features

4 Create a PIN to use when using Kids Home.

If you have already set the screen lock method on your device, you can use the same lock method for Kids Home.

The Kids Home screen will appear.

The created PIN will be used when activating the **Parental control** feature or closing Kids Home.

Using Kids Home

Open the notification panel, swipe downwards on the notification panel, and then tap (**Kids Home**) to activate it.

The Kids Home screen will appear.

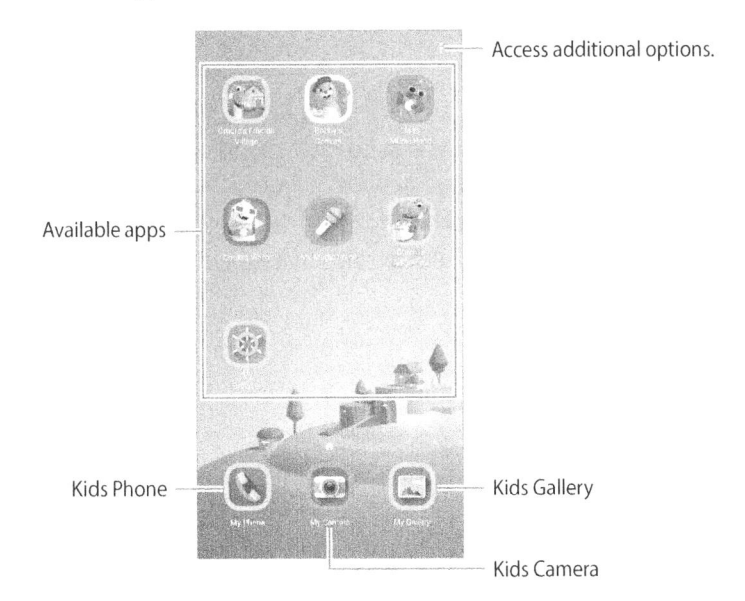

Access additional options.

Available apps

Kids Phone

Kids Gallery

Kids Camera

Configuring settings for Kids Home

On the Kids Home screen, tap → **Parental control** and enter the PIN.

- **Name**: Manage your child's profile.
- **Set daily playtime**: Restrict the usage time for Kids Home.

Apps and features

- **Daily usage**: View the daily usage time of Kids Home.
- **Activity**: View the activity history of Kids Home.
- **Frequently contacted**: View the frequently used contacts in Kids Home.
- **My kid's creations**: View the works created from the apps in Kids Home.
- **Allowed content**: Check the apps or content supported by Kids Home and add them.

Closing Kids Home

To close Kids Home, tap the Back button or tap ⋮ → **Close Kids Home**, and then enter your PIN.

Samsung Pay

Introduction

Register frequently used cards to Samsung Pay, a mobile payment service, to make payments quickly and securely. Samsung Pay supports magnetic secure transmission (MST) as well as near field communication (NFC) to allow payment through standard credit card readers.

You can view more information, such as cards that support this feature at www.samsung.com/samsungpay.

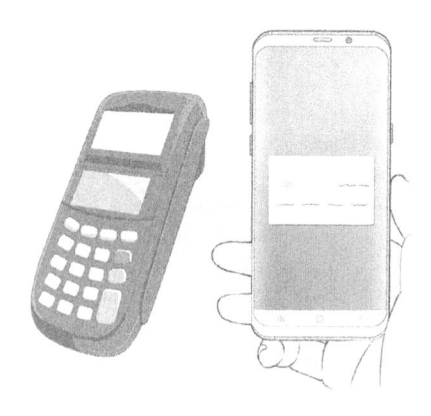

Apps and features

- To use this feature, you must sign in to your Samsung account and register your biometric data. For more information, refer to Samsung account, Fingerprint recognition, and Iris recognition.
- To make payments with Samsung Pay, the device may be required a connection to a Wi-Fi or mobile network depending on the region.
- This app's availability and supported features may vary depending on the region or service provider.
- The procedures for the initial setup and card registration may vary depending on the region or service provider.
- Magnetic secure transmission (MST) may not be supported depending on the region.

Setting up Samsung Pay

When running this app for the first time or restart it after performing a data reset, follow the on-screen instructions to complete the initial setup.

1 Launch the **Samsung Pay** app.

2 Sign in to your Samsung account.

3 Read and agree to the terms and conditions.

4 Register your fingerprint or irises to use when making payments.

5 Create a PIN to use when making payments.

This PIN will be used to verify various actions in Samsung Pay, such as making payments and unlocking the app.

Registering cards

You can easily register cards by capturing their images with the camera.

You can check the cards that support this feature from the Samsung Pay website (www.samsung.com/samsungpay).

Launch the **Samsung Pay** app, tap **Add**, and then follow the on-screen instructions to complete your card registration.

Apps and features

Making payments

1 Tap and hold a card image at the bottom of the screen and drag it upwards. Alternatively, launch the **Samsung Pay** app.

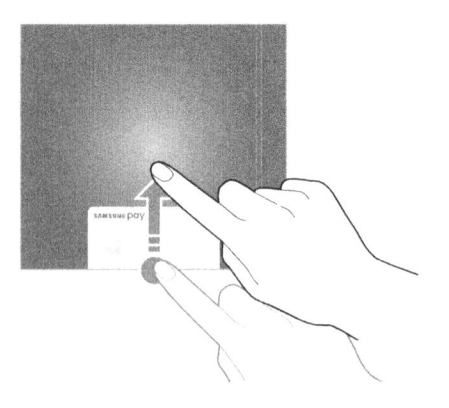

2 On the cards list, swipe to the left or right and select a card to use.

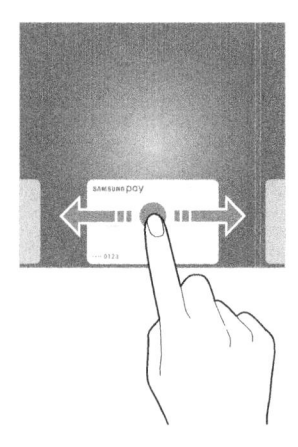

Apps and features

3 Scan your fingerprint or irises.
   Alternatively, enter the payment PIN you set when setting up the Samsung Pay.

4 Touch the back of your device to the card reader.
   When the card reader recognises the card information, the payment will be processed.

- Payments may not be processed depending on your network connection.
- The verification method for payments may vary depending on the card readers.

Cancelling payments

You can cancel payments by visiting the place where you made them.

On the cards list, swipe to the left or right to select the card you used. Follow the on-screen instructions to complete payment cancellation.

Galaxy Wearable

Galaxy Wearable is an app that allows you to manage your wearable devices. When you connect your device to the wearable device, you can customise the wearable device's settings and apps.

Open the **Samsung** folder and launch the **Galaxy Wearable** app.

Tap **START THE JOURNEY** to connect your device to the wearable device. Follow the on-screen instructions to finish the setup. Refer to the wearable device's user manual for more information about how to connect and use the wearable device with your device.

Apps and features

Samsung Members

Samsung Members offers support services to customers, such as device problem diagnosis, and lets users submit questions and error reports. You can also share information with others in the Galaxy users' community or view the latest Galaxy news and tips. **Samsung Members** can help you solve any problems you might encounter while using your device.

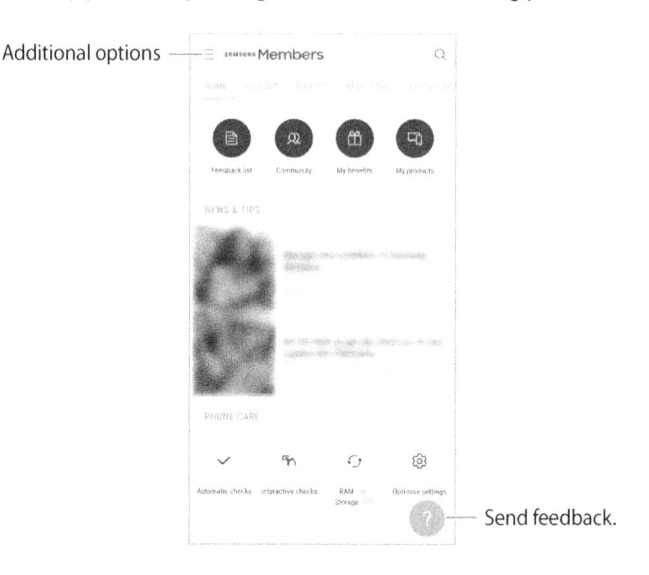

Additional options

Send feedback.

- This app's availability and supported features may vary depending on the region or service provider.
- To submit your feedback or post your comments, you must register and sign in to your Samsung account. Refer to Samsung account for more information.

Apps and features

Samsung Notes

Create notes by entering text from the keyboard or by handwriting or drawing on the screen. You can also insert images or voice recordings into your notes.

Creating notes

1 Launch the **Samsung Notes** app and tap .

2 Select an input method from the toolbar at the top of the screen and compose a note.

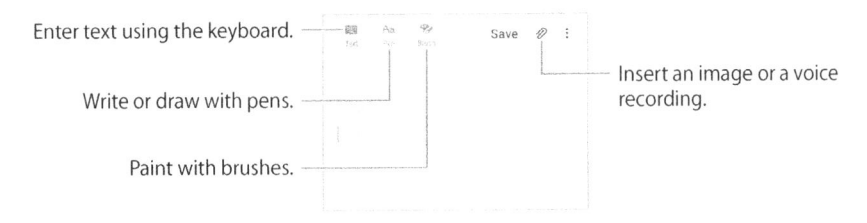

Enter text using the keyboard.
Write or draw with pens.
Paint with brushes.
Save
Insert an image or a voice recording.

3 When you are finished composing the note, tap **Save**.

Deleting notes

1 Launch the **Samsung Notes** app.

2 Tap and hold a note to delete.
To delete multiple notes, tick more notes to delete.

3 Tap **Delete**.

Apps and features

Calendar

Manage your schedule by entering upcoming events or tasks in your planner.

Creating events

1 Launch the **Calendar** app and tap ⊕ or double-tap a date.

If the date already has saved events or tasks in it, tap the date and tap ⊕.

2 Enter event details.

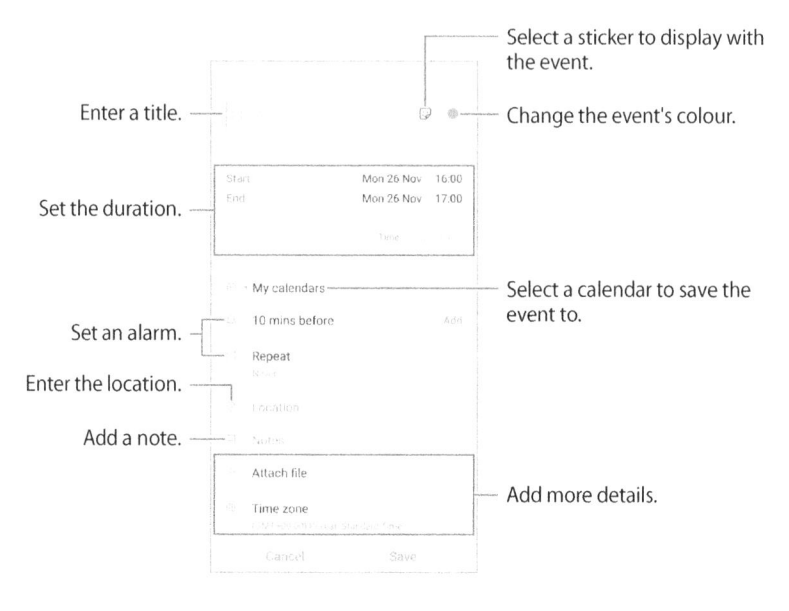

Enter a title.
Set the duration.
Set an alarm.
Enter the location.
Add a note.

Select a sticker to display with the event.
Change the event's colour.
Select a calendar to save the event to.
Add more details.

3 Tap **Save** to save the event.

Apps and features

Adding a reminder

Launch the **Calendar** app and tap ≡ → **Reminder** to launch the **Reminder** app. Add a task on the **Reminder** app. Refer to Reminder for more information.

Syncing events with your accounts

1 Launch the **Settings** app, tap **Accounts and backup** → **Accounts** and select the account to sync with.

2 Tap **Sync account** and tap the **Calendar** switch to activate it.

   For the Samsung account, tap ⋮ → **Sync settings** and tap the **Calendar** switch to activate it.

To add accounts to sync with, launch the **Calendar** app and tap ≡ → ⚙ → **Add new account**. Then, select an account to sync with and sign in. When an account is added, it will appear on the list.

Samsung Health

Introduction

Samsung Health helps you manage your wellness and fitness. Set fitness goals, check your progress, and keep track of your overall wellness and fitness. You can also compare your step count records with other Samsung Health users, compete with your friends, and view health tips.

Apps and features

Using Samsung Health

Open the **Samsung** folder and launch the **Samsung Health** app. When running this app for the first time or restart it after performing a data reset, follow the on-screen instructions to complete the setup.

> Some features may not be available depending on the region.

To add items to the Samsung Health home screen, tap → **Manage items**, and then select items.

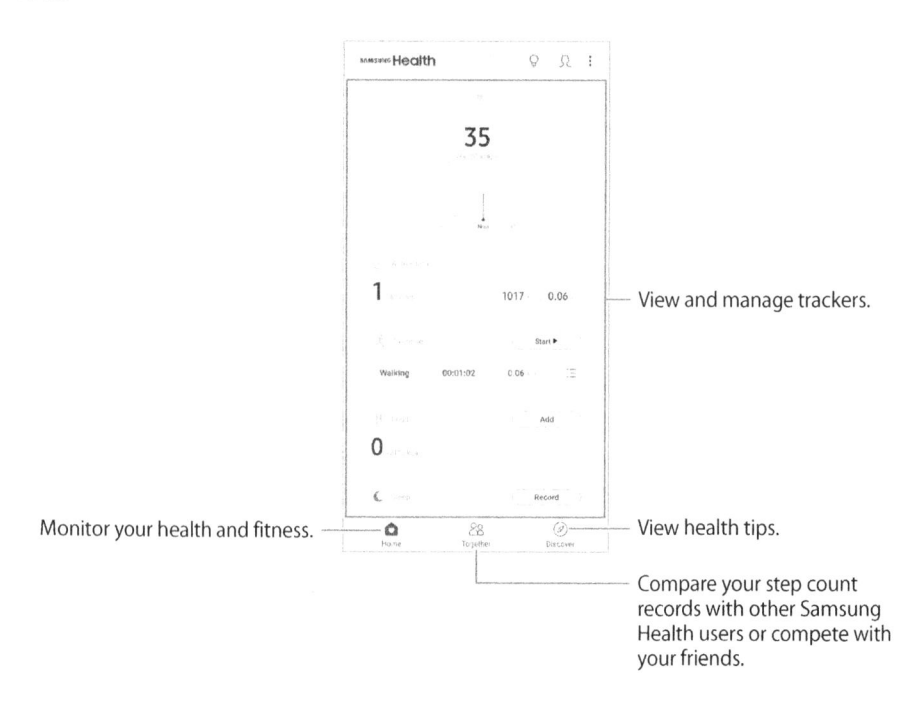

View and manage trackers.

Monitor your health and fitness.

View health tips.

Compare your step count records with other Samsung Health users or compete with your friends.

Apps and features

Together

Together allows you to set up step count goals and compete with your friends. You can invite friends to walk together, set target step counts, compete in challenges, and view your ranking.

On the Samsung Health home screen, tap **Together**.

Steps

The device counts the number of steps you take and measures the distance travelled.

On the Samsung Health home screen, tap the steps tracker.

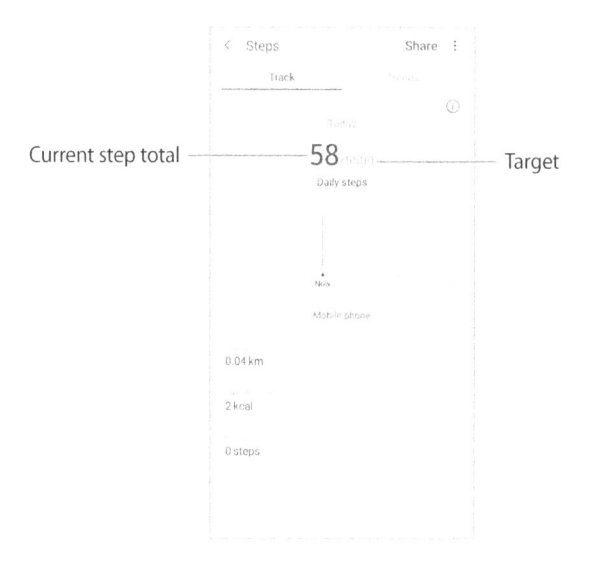

Current step total — 58 — Target

- You may experience a brief delay while the steps tracker monitors your steps a then displays your step count. You may also experience a brief delay before t' pop-up window indicates that your goal has been reached.
- If you use the steps tracker while travelling by car or train, vibration may a' step count.
- You can check your current steps on the notification panel. To turn off on the Samsung Health home screen, tap ⋮ → **Settings** → **Notificatio** tap the **Current steps** switch under **Ongoing** to deactivate it. Altern the notification panel, tap and hold the notification, and then tap t' deactivate it.

157

Heart rate

Measure and record your heart rate.

> The heart rate tracker is intended for fitness and informational purposes only and is not intended for use in the diagnosis of disease or other conditions, or in the cure, mitigation, treatment, or prevention of disease.

Be aware of following conditions before measuring your heart rate:

- Rest for 5 minutes before taking measurements.
- If the measurement is very different from the expected heart rate, rest for 30 minutes and then measure it again.
- During winter or in cold weather, keep yourself warm when measuring your heart rate.
- Smoking or consuming alcohol before taking measurements may cause your heart rate to be different from your normal heart rate.
- Do not talk, yawn, or breathe deeply while taking heart rate measurements. Doing so may cause your heart rate to be recorded inaccurately.
- Heart rate measurements may vary depending on the measurement method and the environment they are taken in.
- If the heart rate sensor is not working, make sure nothing is obstructing the sensor. If the heart rate sensor continues to have the same problem, visit a Samsung Service Centre.

Apps and features

1. On the Samsung Health home screen, tap **Measure** on the heart rate tracker to start measuring your heart rate.

2. Place your finger on the heart rate sensor on the back of the device.

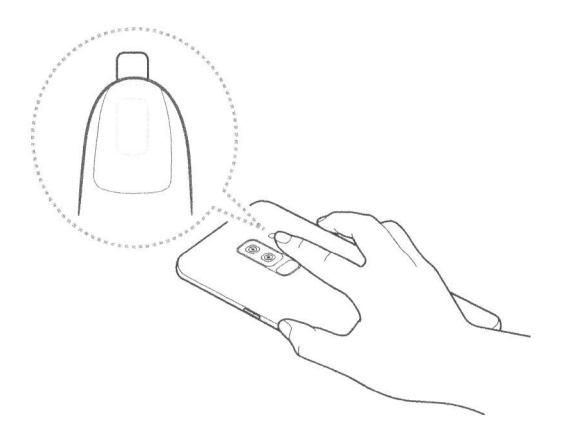

3. After a moment, your current heart rate will be displayed on the screen. Remove your finger from the sensor.

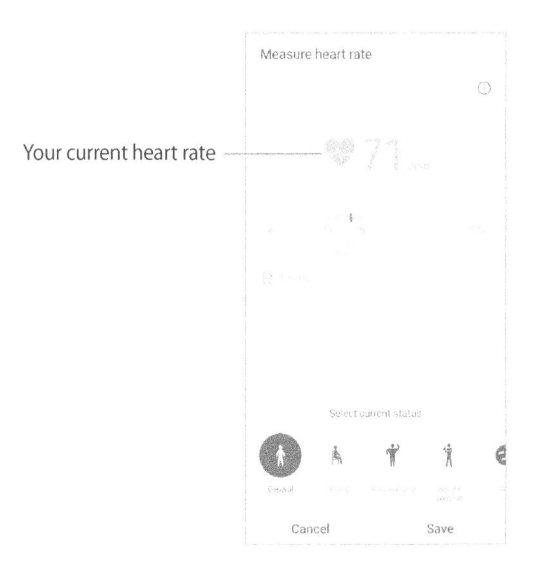

Your current heart rate

Apps and features

Additional information

- Samsung Health is intended for fitness and wellness purposes only and is not intended for use in the diagnosis of disease or other conditions, or in the cure, mitigation, treatment, or prevention of disease.
- The available functions, features and addable applications for Samsung Health may vary from country to country due to different local laws and regulations. You should check the features and applications available in your specific region before use.
- Samsung Health applications and its service can be changed or discontinued without prior notice.
- The purpose for data collection is limited to providing the service that you have requested, including providing additional information to enhance your wellness, sync data, data analysis and statistics or to develop and provide better services. (But if you sign in to your Samsung account from Samsung Health, your data may be saved on the server for data backup purposes.) Personal information may be stored until the completion of such purposes. You can delete personal data stored by Samsung Health by using the Erase personal data option in the Settings menu. To delete any data you have shared with social networks or transferred to storage devices, you must delete them separately.
- You may share and/or sync your data with additional Samsung services or compatible third party services that you select, as well as with any of your other connected devices. Access to Samsung Health information by such additional services or third party devices will only be permitted with your express approval.
- You assume full responsibility for the inappropriate use of data shared on social networks or transmitted to others. Use caution when sharing your personal data with others.
- If the device is connected to measuring devices, verify the communication protocol to confirm proper operation. If you use a wireless connection, such as Bluetooth, the device may be affected by electronic interference from other devices. Avoid using the device near other devices that transmit radio waves.
- Please read Terms and Conditions and Privacy Policy of Samsung Health carefully before using it.

160

Apps and features

Voice Recorder

Introduction

Use different recording modes for various situations. The device can convert your voice to text and distinguish between sound sources.

Making voice recordings

1 Open the **Samsung** folder and launch the **Voice Recorder** app.

2 Tap to start recording. Speak into the microphone.

Tap to pause recording.

While making a voice recording, tap **BOOKMARK** to insert a bookmark.

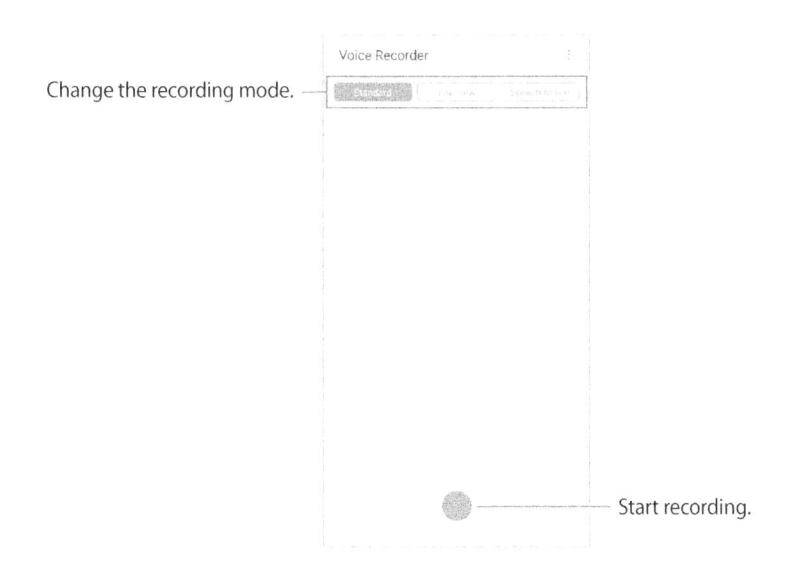

Change the recording mode.

Start recording.

3 Tap to finish recording.

4 Enter a file name and tap **Save**.

161

Apps and features

Changing the recording mode

Open the **Samsung** folder and launch the **Voice Recorder** app.

Select a mode from the top of the voice recorder screen.

- **Standard**: This is the normal recording mode.
- **Interview**: The device records sound from the top and the bottom of the device at a high volume while reducing the volume of sound from the sides.
- **Speech-to-text**: The device records your voice and simultaneously converts it to on-screen text. For best results, keep the device near your mouth and speak loudly and clearly in a quiet place.

> If the voice memo system language does not match the language you are speaking, the device will not recognise your voice. Before using this feature, tap the current language to set the voice memo system language.

Playing selected voice recordings

When you review interview recordings, you can mute or unmute certain sound sources in the recording.

1 Open the **Samsung** folder and launch the **Voice Recorder** app.

2 Tap **List** and select a voice recording made in interview mode.

3 To mute certain sound sources, tap ON for the corresponding direction that sound is to be muted.

The icon will change to OFF and the sound will be muted.

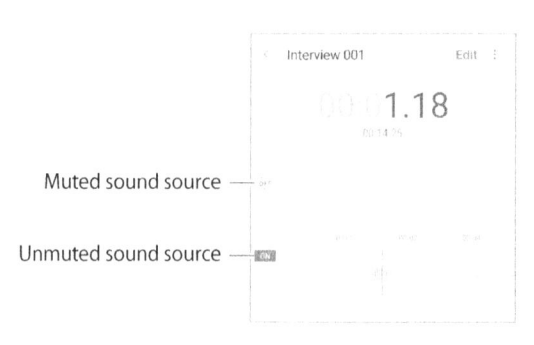

Muted sound source

Unmuted sound source

Apps and features

My Files

Access and manage various files stored in the device or in other locations, such as cloud storage services.

Open the **Samsung** folder and launch the **My Files** app.

View files that are stored in each storage.

To check for unnecessary data and free up the device's storage, tap ⋮ → **Storage analysis**.

To search for files or folders, tap Q.

Clock

Introduction

Set alarms, check the current time in many cities around the world, time an event, or set a specific duration.

Alarm

Launch the **Clock** app and tap **Alarm**.

Setting alarms

Tap ╋ in the alarms list, set an alarm time, select the days on which the alarm will repeat, set other various alarm options, and then tap **Save**.

To open the keypad to enter an alarm time, tap the time input field.

To activate or deactivate alarms, tap the switch next to the alarm in the alarms list.

Stopping alarms

Tap **Dismiss** to stop an alarm. If you have previously enabled the snooze option, tap **Snooze** to repeat the alarm after a specified length of time.

163

Apps and features

Deleting alarms

Tap and hold an alarm, tick alarms to delete, and then tap **Delete**.

World Clock

Launch the **Clock** app and tap **World Clock**.

Creating clocks

Tap ➕, enter a city name or select a city from the map, and then tap **Add**.

To use the time zone converter, tap ⋮ → **Time zone converter**.

Deleting clocks

Tap and hold a clock, tick clocks to delete, and then tap **Delete**.

Stopwatch

1. Launch the **Clock** app and tap **Stopwatch**.

2. Tap **Start** to time an event.
   To record lap times while timing an event, tap **Lap**.

3. Tap **Stop** to stop timing.
   To restart the timing, tap **Resume**.
   To clear lap times, tap **Reset**.

Timer

1. Launch the **Clock** app and tap **Timer**.
   To add a frequently used timer, tap , set the duration and name, and then tap **Add**.

2. Set the duration, and then tap **Start**.
   To open the keypad to enter the duration, tap the duration input field.

3. Tap **Dismiss** when the timer goes off.

Calculator

Perform simple or complex calculations.
Launch the **Calculator** app.
Tap to display the scientific calculator.
To see the calculation history, tap . To close the calculation history panel, tap .
To clear the history, tap → **Clear history**.
To use the unit conversion tool, tap . You can convert various values, such as area, length, or temperature, into other units.

Apps and features

Game Launcher

Introduction

Game Launcher gathers your games downloaded from **Play Store** and **Galaxy Apps** into one place for easy access. You can set the device to game mode to play games more easily.

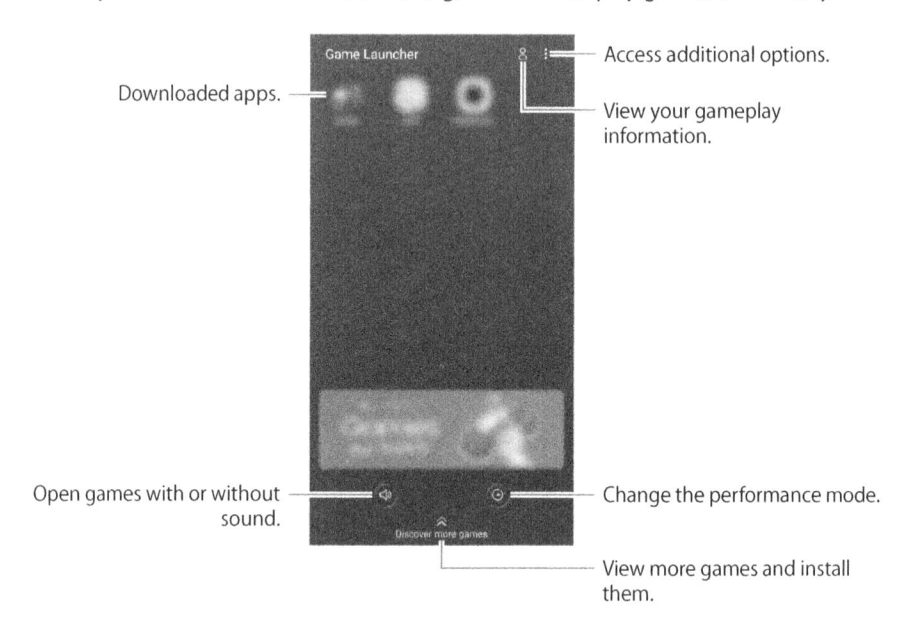

Downloaded apps.

Access additional options.

View your gameplay information.

Open games with or without sound.

Change the performance mode.

View more games and install them.

Using Game Launcher

1 Launch the **Game Launcher** app.

If **Game Launcher** does not appear, launch the **Settings** app, tap **Advanced features**, and then tap the **Game Launcher** switch to activate it.

2 Tap a game from the games list.
To find more games, drag the screen upwards.

Games downloaded from **Play Store** and **Galaxy Apps** will be automatically shown on the game launcher screen. If you cannot see your games, tap ⋮ → **Add apps**.

Removing a game from Game Launcher

Tap and hold a game and tap **Remove**.

Changing the performance mode

You can change the game performance mode.
Launch the **Game Launcher** app, tap , and then drag the bar to select the mode you want.

- **Focus on power saving**: This saves battery power while playing games.
- **Balanced**: This balances the performance and the battery usage time.
- **Focus on performance**: This focuses on giving you the best possible performance while playing games.

To change the settings for each game, tap the **Individual game settings** switch to activate it.

Battery power efficiency may vary by game.

Apps and features

Using Game Tools

You can use various options on the Game Tools panel while playing a game. To open the Game Tools panel, tap ⊙ on the navigation bar. If the navigation bar is hidden, drag upwards from the bottom of the screen to show it.

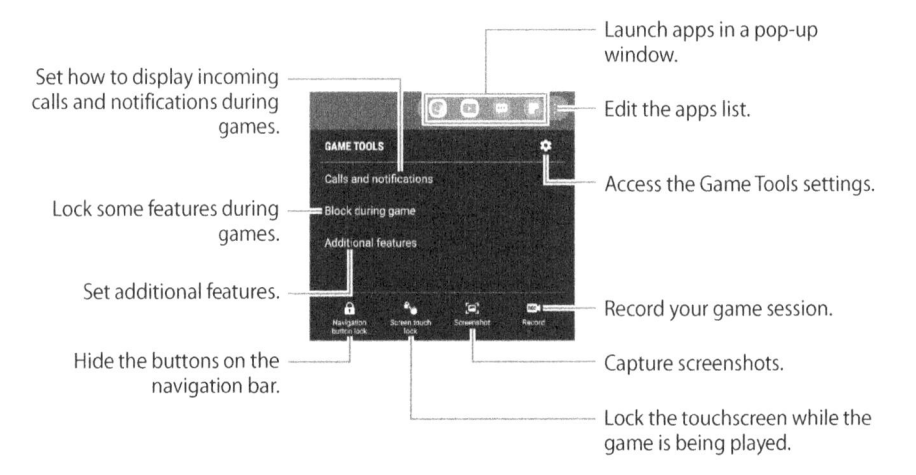

Set how to display incoming calls and notifications during games.

Lock some features during games.

Set additional features.

Hide the buttons on the navigation bar.

Launch apps in a pop-up window.

Edit the apps list.

Access the Game Tools settings.

Record your game session.

Capture screenshots.

Lock the touchscreen while the game is being played.

Available options may vary depending on the game.

Setting how to display incoming calls and notifications during games

You can enjoy your games without being disturbed even when you receive a call or notification.

Tap ⊙ → **Calls and notifications** and select an option to activate it.

- **Minimised caller notifications**: A small notification will appear at the top of the screen when you receive a call during games.
- **Don't display notifications**: Only display notifications from some apps or emergency notifications during games.

Apps and features

SmartThings

Introduction

Connect to nearby devices, such as Bluetooth headsets or other smartphones, easily and quickly. You can also control and manage TVs, home appliances, and Internet of Things (IoT) products with your smartphone.

- **Connecting with nearby devices**: Connect with nearby devices, such as Bluetooth headsets or wearable devices, easily and quickly.
- **Registering and controlling home appliances, TVs, and IoT products**: Register smart refrigerators, washers, air conditioners, air purifiers, TVs, and Internet of Things (IoT) products on your smartphone, and view their status or control them from your smartphone's screen.
- **Receiving notification**: Receive notifications from connected devices on your smartphone. For example, when the laundry is finished, you can receive a notification on your smartphone.

Open the **Samsung** folder and launch the **SmartThings** app. The dashboard will appear.

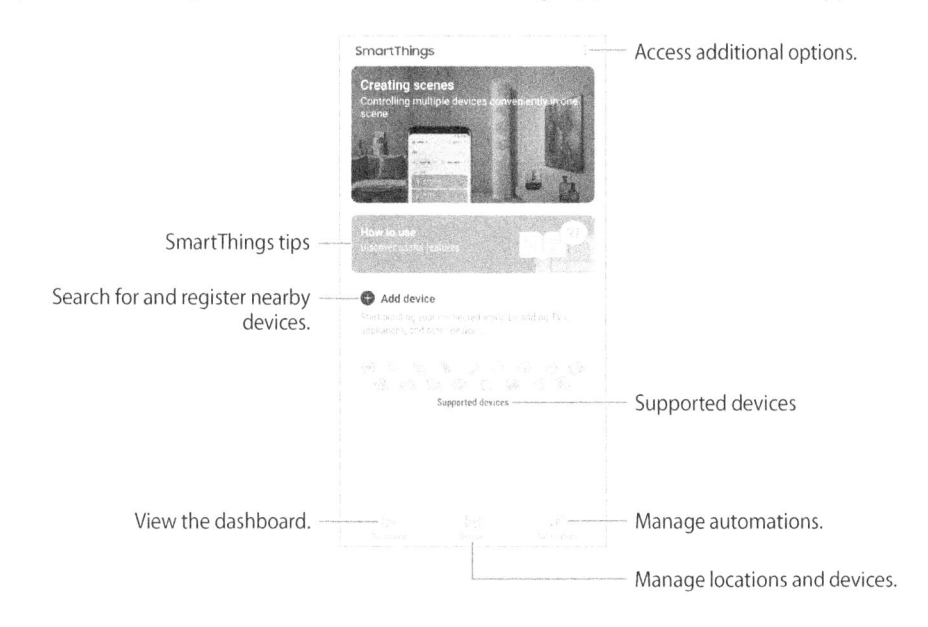

SmartThings tips

Search for and register nearby devices.

Access additional options.

Supported devices

View the dashboard.

Manage automations.

Manage locations and devices.

Apps and features

- To use SmartThings, your smartphone and other devices must be connected to a Wi-Fi or mobile network.
- To fully use SmartThings, you must register and sign in to your Samsung account.
- The devices you can connect may vary depending on the region or service provider. To see the list of connectable devices, open the **Samsung** folder, launch the **SmartThings** app, and then tap **Supported devices**.
- Available features may differ depending on the connected device.
- Connected devices' own errors or defects are not covered by the Samsung warranty. When errors or defects occur on the connected devices, contact the device's manufacturer.

Connecting to nearby devices

Connect to nearby devices, such as Bluetooth headsets, easily and quickly.

- Connection methods may vary depending on the type of connected devices or the shared content.

1 Open the **Samsung** folder and launch the **SmartThings** app.

2 On the dashboard, tap **Add device**.

3 Select a device from the list and connect to it by following the on-screen instructions.

170

Apps and features

Using home appliances, TVs, and IoT products

View the status of your smart appliances, TVs, and IoT products from your smartphone's screen. You can group devices by location and add rules to control the devices easily and conveniently.

Connecting devices

1 Open the **Samsung** folder and launch the **SmartThings** app.

2 On the dashboard, tap **Add device**.

3 Select a device from the list.

If there is no device on the list, tap ⌄ under **ADD DEVICE MANUALLY** and select a device type. Or, tap **Search** and enter the device or model name.

4 Follow the on-screen instructions to register devices.

Viewing and controlling connected devices

You can view and control the devices. For example, you can check the ingredients in your refrigerator or adjust the TV volume.

1 Open the **Samsung** folder, launch the **SmartThings** app.

The list of connected devices will appear.

2 View the status of devices on the list.

To control the devices, select a device. When the device controller supplied with the selected device is downloaded, you can control the device.

Apps and features

Adding devices and scenes by locations

Add devices by locations, view the list of devices in a same location, and control them. You can also add a scene to a location to control multiple devices at the same time.

Adding locations

1 Open the **Samsung** folder, launch the **SmartThings** app, and then tap **Devices** → **ALL DEVICES** → **Add location**.

2 Enter the location name.

 To set a location, tap **Geolocation** to select a location on the map and tap **DONE**.

3 Tap **SAVE**.

 Your location will be added.

 To add devices to the location, tap **ADD DEVICE** and follow the on-screen instructions to register devices.

 The devices will be added to the location.

Adding scenes

Add a scene and register devices to it to control multiple devices at the same time with a single tap of a button or with a voice command.

Open the **Samsung** folder, launch the **SmartThings** app, select a location, tap → **Add scene**, and then set scene options. You can set the scene name, icon, and devices.

Apps and features

Adding automations

You can also set an automation to operate devices automatically depending on the preset time, the status of devices, and more.

For example, add an automation to turn on the audio automatically every day at 7:00 AM.

1 Open the **Samsung** folder, launch the **SmartThings** app, and then tap **Automations** → **ADD AUTOMATION**.

2 Select the location to run the automation.

3 Set the activation conditions for this automation.

4 Tap **ADD** next to **Then** and set actions to perform.

5 Tap **SAVE**.

Receiving notifications

You can receive notifications from connected devices on your smartphone. For example, when the laundry is finished, you can receive a notification on your smartphone.

To set devices to receive notifications, open the **Samsung** folder, launch the **SmartThings** app, tap → **Settings** → **Notifications**, and then tap the switches next to the devices you want.

Apps and features

Sharing content

Share content by using various sharing options. The following actions are an example of sharing images.

> You may incur additional charges when sharing files via the mobile network.

1 Launch the **Gallery** app and select an image.

2 Tap ⊰ and select a sharing method, such as message and email.

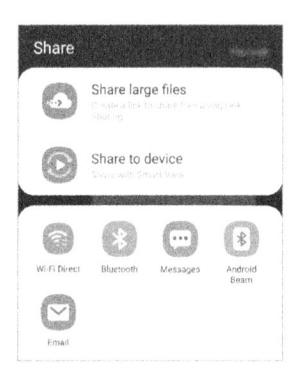

> When you have a communication or sharing history, the people you contacted will appear on the sharing options panel. To directly share content with them via the corresponding app, select a person's icon. If the feature is not activated, launch the **Settings** app, tap **Advanced features**, and then tap the **Direct share** switch to activate it.

Using additional features

- **Share large files**: Share large files. Upload files to the Samsung storage server and share them with others via a Web link or a code. To use this feature, your phone number must be verified.
- **Share to device**: Share content with nearby devices via Wi-Fi Direct or Bluetooth, or with SmartThings supported devices. You can also view your device's displayed content on a large screen by connecting your device to a screen mirroring-enabled TV or monitor.

When the image is sent to the recipients' devices, a notification will appear on their devices. Tap the notification to view or download the image.

Apps and features

Samsung DeX

Introduction

Samsung DeX is a service that allows you to use your smartphone like a computer by connecting the smartphone to an external display, such as a TV or monitor. While using Samsung DeX, you can simultaneously use your smartphone.

You can connect your smartphone to an external display using an HDMI adaptor (USB Type-C to HDMI) or DeX Pad. The following content is about how to use the HDMI adaptor.

- All accessories are sold separately.
- Use only official Samsung DeX supported accessories that are provided by Samsung. Performance problems and malfunctions caused by using accessories that are not officially supported are not covered by the warranty.

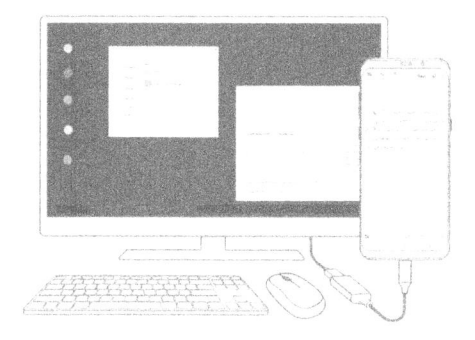

Apps and features

Starting Samsung DeX

1 Connect an HDMI adaptor to your smartphone.

2 Connect an HDMI cable to the HDMI adaptor and to a TV or monitor's HDMI port.

3 On your smartphone's screen, tap **Continue** → **Start**.

Without changing your smartphone's screen, the Samsung DeX screen will appear on the connected TV or monitor.

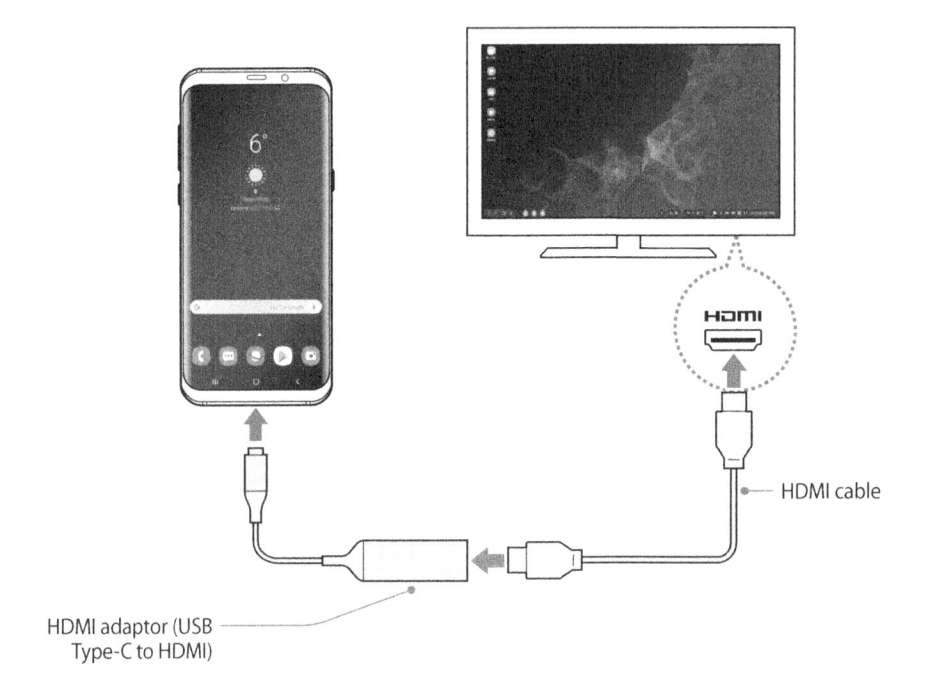

HDMI cable

HDMI adaptor (USB Type-C to HDMI)

Apps and features

Controlling the Samsung DeX screen

Controlling with an external keyboard and mouse

You can use a wireless keyboard/mouse. Refer to the respective device's manual for more information.

- You can set the mouse pointer to flow from the external display to the smartphone's screen. Launch the **Settings** app, select **Samsung DeX** → **Mouse/trackpad**, and then select the **Flow pointer to phone screen** switch to activate it.
- You can also use the external keyboard on the smartphone's screen.

Using your smartphone as a touchpad

You can use your smartphone as a touchpad and operate it with your fingers.

On your smartphone, drag downwards from the top of the screen to open the notification panel and tap **Use your phone as a touchpad**.

- You can use the touchpad only when using Samsung DeX mode.
- If your smartphone's case has a front cover, open the front cover to use your smartphone as a touchpad. If the front cover is closed, the touchpad may not work properly.
- If your smartphone's screen turns off, press the Power key to turn on the screen.

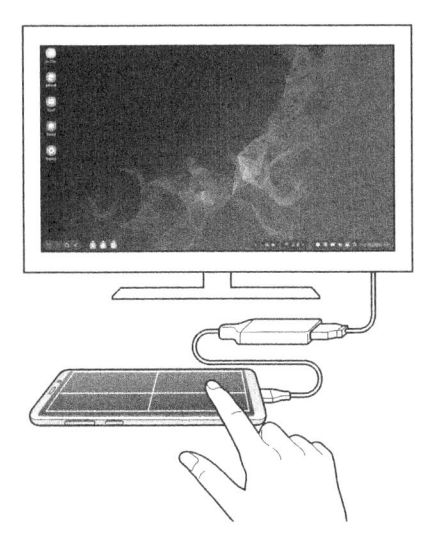

Apps and features

Orienting the touchpad

When you are using your smartphone as a touchpad, you can use it in either the horizontal or vertical alignment.

To rotate the touchpad, rotate the smartphone or double-tap .

Using your smartphone while using the touchpad

On your smartphone, drag upwards from the bottom of the screen to show the navigation bar. Then, tap the Home button to move to the Home screen and select the apps you want to use.

Using the screen keyboard

When you enter text to send messages, create notes, or perform other tasks, a screen keyboard will appear automatically on your smartphone's screen without connecting an external keyboard.

If the keyboard does not appear, select on the quick access toolbar.

Apps and features

Using Samsung DeX

Use your smartphone's features in an interface environment similar to a computer. You can multitask by running multiple apps simultaneously. You can also check your smartphone's notifications and status.

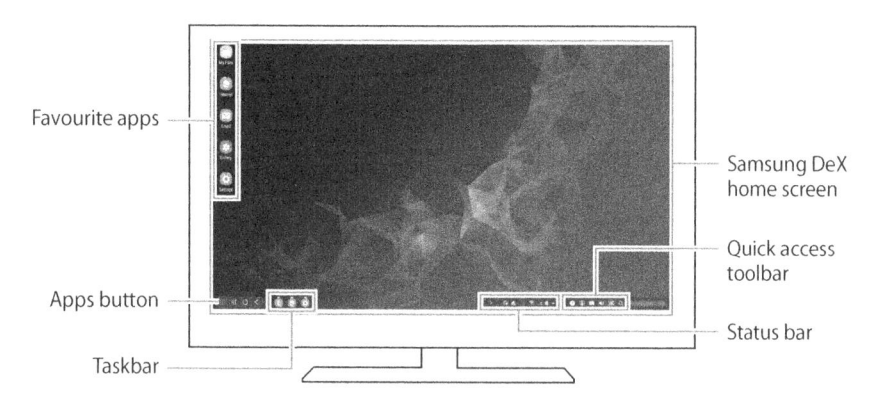

Favourite apps

Samsung DeX home screen

Quick access toolbar

Apps button

Status bar

Taskbar

- When starting or ending Samsung DeX, running apps may be closed.
- Some apps or features may not be available when using Samsung DeX.
- To adjust the screen settings, use the connected TV or monitor's display settings.
- Sound will be played through the smartphone's speaker. To change the default audio output, launch the **Settings** app, select **Samsung DeX**, and then select the **Set default audio output** switch to activate it.

- Favourite apps: Add frequently used apps to the Home screen and launch them quickly.
- Apps button: View and run your smartphone's apps. To install apps that are optimised for Samsung DeX, select **Apps for Samsung DeX**.
- Taskbar: View the apps that are currently running.
- Status bar: View your smartphone's notifications and status. Status icons may appear differently depending on your smartphone's status. When you select ▲, the quick setting buttons will appear. You can activate or deactivate certain smartphone features using the quick setting buttons.

  To switch to screen mirroring mode, select ⌂ → **Screen mirroring**.
- Quick access toolbar: Use quick tools, such as screen keyboard, volume control, or search.

Using the external display and smartphone simultaneously

While using Samsung DeX, you can use separate apps on the external display and your smartphone simultaneously.

For example, while watching a video on the connected TV or monitor, you can create a note on your smartphone.

On the connected TV or monitor, launch an app to run on the Samsung DeX screen. Then, launch another app on your smartphone.

Locking the Samsung DeX screen

If you want to lock the external display and your smartphone's screen while using Samsung DeX, select ![icon] on the quick access toolbar.

> While using Samsung DeX, you cannot lock the external display and your smartphone's screen by pressing the Power key.

Enjoying games vividly on a large screen

Play your smartphone's games on a large screen. On the connected TV or monitor, launch the **Game Launcher** app.

Ending Samsung DeX

When you disconnect your smartphone from the connected TV or monitor, Samsung DeX will end.

Disconnect your smartphone from the HDMI adaptor.

Apps and features

Google apps

Google provides entertainment, social network, and business apps. You may require a Google account to access some apps.

To view more app information, access each app's help menu.

Some apps may not be available or may be labelled differently depending on the region or service provider.

Chrome

Search for information and browse webpages.

Gmail

Send or receive emails via the Google Mail service.

Maps

Find your location on the map, search the world map, and view location information for various places around you.

Play Music

Discover, listen to, and share music on your device. You can upload music collections stored on your device to the cloud and access them later.

Play Movies & TV

Purchase or rent videos, such as movies and TV programmes, from **Play Store**.

Drive

Store your content on the cloud, access it from anywhere, and share it with others.

Apps and features

YouTube

Watch or create videos and share them with others.

Photos

Search for, manage, and edit all your photos and videos from various sources in one place.

Google

Search quickly for items on the Internet or your device.

Duo

Make a simple video call.

Settings

Introduction

Customise device settings. You can make your device more personalised by configuring various setting options.

Launch the **Settings** app.

To search for settings by entering keywords, tap Q.

Connections

Options

Change settings for various connections, such as the Wi-Fi feature and Bluetooth.

On the Settings screen, tap **Connections**.

- **Wi-Fi**: Activate the Wi-Fi feature to connect to a Wi-Fi network and access the Internet or other network devices. Refer to Wi-Fi for more information.

- **Bluetooth**: Use Bluetooth to exchange data or media files with other Bluetooth-enabled devices. Refer to Bluetooth for more information.

- **Phone visibility**: Allow other devices to find your device to share content with you. When this feature is activated, your device will be visible to other devices when they search for available devices using their Transfer files to device option.

- **NFC and payment**: Set the device to allow you to read near field communication (NFC) tags that contain information about products. You can also use this feature to make payments and buy tickets for transportation or events after downloading the required apps. Refer to NFC and payment for more information.

Settings

- **Flight mode**: Set the device to disable all wireless functions on your device. You can use only non-network services.

    Follow the regulations provided by the airline and the instructions of aircraft personnel. In cases where it is allowed to use the device, always use it in flight mode.

- **Mobile networks**: Configure your mobile network settings.
- **Data usage**: Keep track of your data usage amount and customise the settings for the limitation. Set the device to automatically disable the mobile data connection when the amount of mobile data you have used reaches your specified limit.

    You can also activate the data saver feature to prevent some apps running in the background from sending or receiving data. Refer to Data saver for more information.

- **SIM card manager** (dual SIM models): Activate your SIM or USIM cards and customise the SIM card settings. Refer to SIM card manager (dual SIM models) for more information.
- **Mobile Hotspot and Tethering**: Use the device as a mobile hotspot to share the device's mobile data connection with other devices when the network connection is not available. Connections can be made via Wi-Fi, USB, or Bluetooth. Refer to Mobile Hotspot and Tethering for more information.
- **More connection settings**: Customise settings to control other features. Refer to More connection settings for more information.

Wi-Fi

Activate the Wi-Fi feature to connect to a Wi-Fi network and access the Internet or other network devices.

Turn off Wi-Fi to save the battery when not in use.

Settings

Connecting to a Wi-Fi network

1 On the Settings screen, tap **Connections** → **Wi-Fi**, and then tap the switch to activate it.

2 Select a network from the Wi-Fi networks list.

Networks that require a password appear with a lock icon. Enter the password and tap **Connect**.

- Once the device connects to a Wi-Fi network, the device will reconnect to that network each time it is available without requiring a password. To prevent the device connecting to the network automatically, select it from the list of networks and tap **Forget**.
- If you cannot connect to a Wi-Fi network properly, restart your device's Wi-Fi feature or the wireless router.

Wi-Fi Direct

Wi-Fi Direct connects devices directly via a Wi-Fi network without requiring an access point.

1 On the Settings screen, tap **Connections** → **Wi-Fi**, and then tap the switch to activate it.

2 Tap **Wi-Fi Direct**.

The detected devices are listed.

If the device you want to connect to is not in the list, request that the device turns on its Wi-Fi Direct feature.

3 Select a device to connect to.

The devices will be connected when the other device accepts the Wi-Fi Direct connection request.

Settings

Sending and receiving data

You can share data, such as contacts or media files, with other devices. The following actions are an example of sending an image to another device.

1 Launch the **Gallery** app and select an image.

2 Tap → **Wi-Fi Direct** and select a device to transfer the image to.

3 Accept the Wi-Fi Direct connection request on the other device.

If the devices are already connected, the image will be sent to the other device without the connection request procedure.

Ending the device connection

1 On the Settings screen, tap **Connections** → **Wi-Fi**.

2 Tap **Wi-Fi Direct**.

The device displays the connected devices in the list.

3 Tap the device name to disconnect the devices.

Settings

Bluetooth

Use Bluetooth to exchange data or media files with other Bluetooth-enabled devices.

- Samsung is not responsible for the loss, interception, or misuse of data sent or received via Bluetooth.
- Always ensure that you share and receive data with devices that are trusted and properly secured. If there are obstacles between the devices, the operating distance may be reduced.
- Some devices, especially those that are not tested or approved by the Bluetooth SIG, may be incompatible with your device.
- Do not use the Bluetooth feature for illegal purposes (for example, pirating copies of files or illegally tapping communications for commercial purposes). Samsung is not responsible for the repercussion of illegal use of the Bluetooth feature.

Pairing with other Bluetooth devices

1 On the Settings screen, tap **Connections** → **Bluetooth**, and then tap the switch to activate it.

The detected devices will be listed.

2 Select a device to pair with.

If the device you want to pair with is not on the list, set the device to enter Bluetooth pairing mode. Refer to the other device's user manuals.

Your device is visible to other devices while the Bluetooth settings screen is open.

3 Accept the Bluetooth connection request on your device to confirm.

The devices will be connected when the other device accepts the Bluetooth connection request.

Settings

Sending and receiving data

Many apps support data transfer via Bluetooth. You can share data, such as contacts or media files, with other Bluetooth devices. The following actions are an example of sending an image to another device.

1 Launch the **Gallery** app and select an image.

2 Tap ⤳ → **Bluetooth**, and then select a device to transfer the image to.

   If your device has paired with the device before, tap the device name without confirming the auto-generated passkey.

   If the device you want to pair with is not in the list, request that the device turns on its visibility option.

3 Accept the Bluetooth connection request on the other device.

Dual audio

You can connect up to two Bluetooth audio devices to your smartphone. Connect two Bluetooth headsets or speakers to use them at the same time.

> To use this feature, the Bluetooth audio devices you want to connect must support the **Media audio** feature.

1 On the Settings screen, tap **Connections** → **Bluetooth**, and then tap the switch to activate it.

   The detected devices will be listed.

2 Tap ⋮ → **Advanced**, tap the **Dual audio** switch to activate it, and then tap the Back button.

Settings

3 Select a device to pair with.

If the device you want to pair with is not in the list, turn on its visibility option or enter Bluetooth pairing mode on the device. Refer to the device's user manuals for more information.

4 Tap next to the connected device and tap the **Media audio** switch to activate it.

5 Select another device from the list and activate its **Media audio** feature.

Unpairing Bluetooth devices

1 On the Settings screen, tap **Connections** → **Bluetooth**.

The device displays the paired devices in the list.

2 Tap next to the device name to unpair.

3 Tap **Unpair**.

NFC and payment

Your device allows you to read near field communication (NFC) tags that contain information about products. You can also use this feature to make payments and buy tickets for transportation or events after downloading the required apps.

The device contains a built-in NFC antenna. Handle the device carefully to avoid damaging the NFC antenna.

Settings

Reading information from NFC tags

Use the NFC feature to send images or contacts to other devices, and read product information from NFC tags.

1 On the Settings screen, tap **Connections** and tap the **NFC and payment** switch to activate it.

2 Place the NFC antenna area on the back of your device near an NFC tag.
The information from the tag appears.

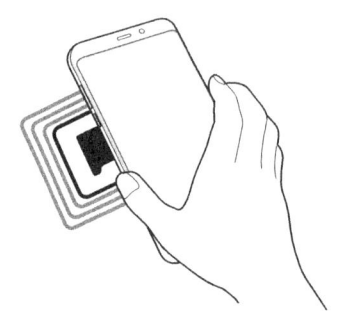

Ensure that the device's screen is turned on and unlocked. Otherwise, the device will not read NFC tags or receive data.

Settings

Making payments with the NFC feature

Before you can use the NFC feature to make payments, you must register for the mobile payment service. To register or get more information about the service, contact your service provider.

1 On the Settings screen, tap **Connections** and tap the **NFC and payment** switch to activate it.

2 Touch the NFC antenna area on the back of your device to the NFC card reader.

To set the default payment app, open the Settings screen and tap **Connections** → **NFC and payment** → **Tap and pay** → **PAYMENT**, and then select an app.

The payment services list may not include all available payment apps.

Sending data with the NFC feature

Allow data exchange when your device's NFC antenna touches the other device's NFC antenna.

1 On the Settings screen, tap **Connections** → **NFC and payment** and tap the switch to activate it.

2 Tap the **Android Beam** switch to activate it.

3 Select an item and touch the other device's NFC antenna to your device's NFC antenna.

Settings

4. When **Touch to beam.** appears on the screen, tap your device's screen to send the item.

If both devices try to send data simultaneously, the file transfer may fail.

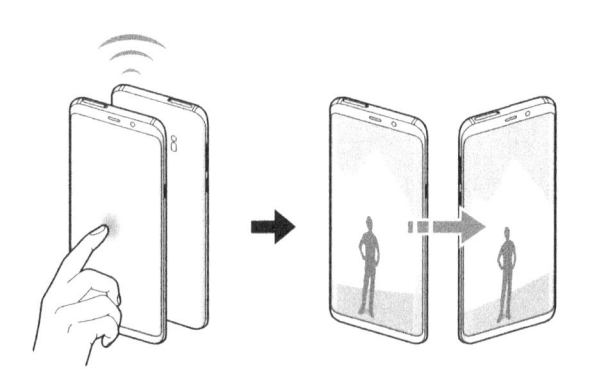

Data saver

Reduce your data usage by preventing some apps running in the background from sending or receiving data.

On the Settings screen, tap **Connections** → **Data usage** → **Data saver** and tap the switch to activate it.

When the data saver feature is activated, the icon will appear on the status bar.

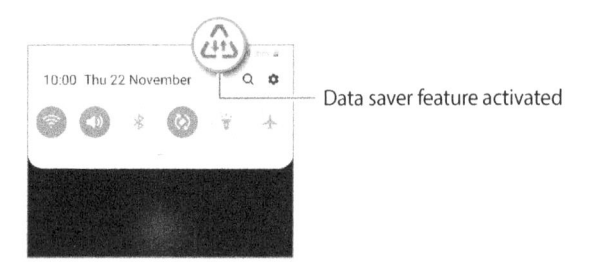

Data saver feature activated

To select apps to use data without restriction, tap **Allow app while Data saver on** and select apps.

Settings

SIM card manager (dual SIM models)

Activate your SIM or USIM cards and customise the SIM card settings. Refer to Using dual SIM or USIM cards (dual SIM models) for more information.

On the Settings screen, tap **Connections** → **SIM card manager**.

- **Calls**: Select a SIM or USIM card for voice calls.
- **Text messages**: Select a SIM or USIM card for messaging.
- **Mobile data**: Select a SIM or USIM card for data services.
- **Confirm SIM card for calls**: Set the device to display the SIM or USIM card selection pop-up window when returning a call or calling from a message. The pop-up window will appear only if the SIM or USIM card used for the previous call or message is different from your preferred SIM or USIM card.
- **Dual SIM always on**: Set the device to allow incoming calls from the other SIM or USIM card during a call.

When this feature is enabled, you may incur additional charges for call forwarding depending on the region or service provider.

Mobile Hotspot and Tethering

Use the device as a mobile hotspot to share the device's mobile data connection with other devices when the network connection is not available. Connections can be made via Wi-Fi, USB, or Bluetooth.

On the Settings screen, tap **Connections** → **Mobile Hotspot and Tethering**.

You may incur additional charges when using this feature.

- **Mobile Hotspot**: Use the mobile hotspot to share the device's mobile data connection with computers or other devices.
- **Bluetooth tethering**: Use Bluetooth tethering to share the device's mobile data connection with computers or other devices via Bluetooth.
- **USB tethering**: Use USB tethering to share the device's mobile data connection with a computer via USB. When connected to a computer, the device is used as a wireless modem for the computer.

Settings

Using the mobile hotspot

Use your device as a mobile hotspot to share your device's mobile data connection with other devices.

1 On the Settings screen, tap **Connections** → **Mobile Hotspot and Tethering** → **Mobile Hotspot**.

2 Tap the switch to activate it.

The icon appears on the status bar. Other devices can find your device in the Wi-Fi networks list.

To set a password for the mobile hotspot, tap → **Configure Mobile Hotspot** and select the level of security. Then, enter a password and tap **Save**.

3 On the other device's screen, search for and select your device from the Wi-Fi networks list.

- If the mobile hotspot is not found, on your device, tap → **Configure Mobile Hotspot**, tick **Show advanced options**, and then deselect **Hide my device** and **Use 5 GHz band when available**.
- If the other device cannot connect to the mobile hotspot, on your device, tap → **Allowed devices** and tap the **Allowed devices only** switch to deactivate it.

4 On the connected device, use the device's mobile data connection to access the Internet.

Settings

More connection settings

Customise settings to control other connection features.
On the Settings screen, tap **Connections** → **More connection settings**.

- **Nearby device scanning**: Set the device to scan for nearby devices to connect to.
- **Printing**: Configure settings for printer plug-ins installed on the device. You can search for available printers or add one manually to print files. Refer to Printing for more information.
- **MirrorLink**: Use the MirrorLink feature to control your device's MirrorLink apps on the vehicle's head unit monitor. Refer to MirrorLink for more information.
- **Download booster**: Set the device to download files larger than 30 MB, faster via Wi-Fi and mobile networks simultaneously. Refer to Download booster for more information.
- **VPN**: Set up virtual networks (VPNs) on your device to connect to a school or company's private network.
- **Private DNS**: Use the reliable domain name system (DNS) for a school or company's internal private network instead of using the external hosting network. The DNS will be searched for and connected to automatically, or you can search for the DNS and connect to it manually.
- **Ethernet**: When you connect an Ethernet adaptor, you can use a wired network and configure network settings.

Printing

Configure settings for printer plug-ins installed on the device. You can connect the device to a printer via Wi-Fi or Wi-Fi Direct, and print images or documents.

Some printers may not be compatible with the device.

Adding printer plug-ins

Add printer plug-ins for printers you want to connect the device to.

1 On the Settings screen, tap **Connections** → **More connection settings** → **Printing** → **Download plugin**.

Settings

2 Search for a printer plug-in in **Play Store**.

3 Select a printer plug-in and install it.

4 Select the installed printer plug-in.

The device will automatically search for printers that are connected to the same Wi-Fi network as your device.

5 Select a printer to add.

To add printers manually, tap ⋮ → **Add printer**.

Printing content

While viewing content, such as images or documents, access the options list, tap **Print** → ▼ → **All printers…**, and then select a printer.

Printing methods may vary depending on the content type.

MirrorLink

You can display your device's screen on the vehicle's head unit monitor.

Connect your device to a vehicle to control your device's MirrorLink apps on the vehicle's head unit monitor.

On the Settings screen, tap **Connections** → **More connection settings** → **MirrorLink**.

Your device is compatible with vehicles that support MirrorLink version 1.1 or higher.

Settings

Connecting your device to a vehicle via MirrorLink

When using this feature for the first time, connect the device to a Wi-Fi or mobile network.

1 Pair your device with a vehicle via Bluetooth.

Refer to Pairing with other Bluetooth devices for more information.

2 Connect your device to the vehicle using a USB cable.

When they are connected, access your device's MirrorLink apps on the head unit monitor.

Ending the MirrorLink connection

Unplug the USB cable from your device and the vehicle.

Download booster

Set the device to download files larger than 30 MB, faster via Wi-Fi and mobile networks simultaneously. A stronger Wi-Fi signal will provide a faster download speed.

On the Settings screen, tap **Connections** → **More connection settings** → **Download booster**.

- This feature may not be supported by some devices.
- You may incur additional charges when downloading files via the mobile network.
- When you download large files, the device may heat up. If the device exceeds a set temperature, the feature will turn off.
- If network signals are unstable, the speed and performance of this feature may be affected.
- If the Wi-Fi and mobile network connections have significantly different data transfer speeds, the device may use only the fastest connection.
- This feature supports Hypertext Transmission Protocol (HTTP) 1.1 and Hypertext Transmission Protocol Secure (HTTPS). The feature cannot be used with other protocols, such as FTP.

Settings

Sounds and vibration

Options

Change settings for various sounds on the device.

On the Settings screen, tap **Sounds and vibration**.

- **Sound mode**: Set the device to use sound mode, vibration mode, or silent mode.
- **Vibrate while ringing**: Set the device to vibrate and play a ringtone for incoming calls.
- **Ringtone**: Change the call ringtone.
- **Vibration pattern**: Select a vibration pattern.
- **Notification sounds**: Change the notification sound.
- **Volume**: Adjust the volume level for call ringtones, music and videos, system sounds, and notifications.
- **Vibration intensity**: Adjust the force of the vibration notification.
- **Use Volume keys for media**: Set the device to adjust the media volume level when you press the Volume key.
- **System feedback**: Set the device to sound or vibrate for actions, such as turning the screen on or off or controlling the touchscreen.
- **Advanced sound settings**: Optimise the settings for when media is being played. Refer to Dolby Atmos (surround sound) or Separate app sound for more information.

Dolby Atmos (surround sound)

Select a surround sound mode optimised for various types of audio, such as movies, music, and voice. With Dolby Atmos, you can experience moving audio sounds that flows all around you.

On the Settings screen, tap **Sounds and vibration** → **Advanced sound settings** → **Sound quality and effects** → **Dolby Atmos**, tap the switch to activate it, and then select a mode.

Settings

Separate app sound

Set the device to play media sound from a specific app on the connected Bluetooth speaker or headset separate from the sound of other apps.

For example, you can listen to the Navigation app through your device's speaker while listening to playback from the Music app through the vehicle's Bluetooth speaker.

1 On the Settings screen, tap **Sounds and vibration** → **Advanced sound settings** → **Separate app sound** and tap the switch to activate it.

2 Select an app to play media sounds separately and tap the Back button.

3 Select a device for playing the selected app's media sound.

Notifications

Options

Change the notification settings.

On the Settings screen, tap **Notifications**.

- **App icon badges**: Change the settings for app icon badges. Refer to App icon badges for more information.
- **Do not disturb**: Set the device to mute incoming calls, notification sounds, and media, except for allowed exceptions.
- **Status bar**: Set the device to display only three recent notifications and whether to show the remaining battery level in percentage on the status bar.
- **LED indicator**: Set the device to turn on the LED indicator when you charge the battery, when you have notifications, or when you make voice recordings while the screen is turned off.
- **Recently sent**: View the apps that received recent notifications and change the notification settings. To customise notification settings for more apps, tap **See all** → → **All** and select an app from the app list.

App icon badges

Change the settings for app icon badges.

On the Settings screen, tap **Notifications** → **App icon badges**.

To display icon badges, tap the switch to activate it. To change the badge style, select an option under **Badge style**.

With number Without number

Display

Options

Change the display and the Home screen settings.

On the Settings screen, tap **Display**.

- **Brightness**: Adjust the brightness of the display.
- **Adaptive brightness**: Set the device to keep track of your brightness adjustments and apply them automatically in similar lighting conditions.
- **Blue light filter**: Activate the blue light filter and change the filter settings. Refer to Blue light filter for more information.
- **Night mode**: Reduce eye strain by applying the dark theme when using the device at night or in a dark place.

    - Turn on the GPS feature to set the device to activate night mode at night and turn it off in the morning based on your current location.
    - The dark theme may not be applied in some apps.

Settings

- **Screen mode**: Change the screen mode to adjust the display's colour and contrast. Refer to Changing the screen mode or adjusting the display colour for more information.
- **Font size and style**: Change the font size and style.
- **Screen zoom**: Change the screen zoom setting.
- **Screen resolution**: Change the screen resolution. Refer to Screen resolution for more information.
- **Full screen apps**: Select apps to use with the full screen aspect ratio.
- **Screen timeout**: Set the length of time the device waits before turning off the display's backlight.
- **Home screen**: Change the size of the grid to display more or fewer items on the Home screen and more.
- **Edge screen**: Change the settings for the Edge screen. Refer to Edge screen for more information.
- **Easy mode**: Switch to easy mode to display larger icons and apply a simpler layout to the Home screen.
- **Navigation bar**: Change the navigation bar settings. Refer to Navigation bar (soft buttons) for more information.
- **Accidental touch protection**: Set the device to prevent the screen from detecting touch input when it is in a dark place, such as a pocket or bag.
- **Touch sensitivity**: Increase the touch sensitivity of the screen for use with screen protectors.
- **Screensaver**: Set the device to launch a screensaver when the device is charging. Refer to Screensaver for more information.

Settings

Blue light filter

Reduce eye strain by limiting the amount of blue light emitted by the screen.

> While you are watching HDR videos from HDR-exclusive video services, the blue light filter may not be applied.

1 On the Settings screen, tap **Display** → **Blue light filter**, and then tap the **Turn on now** switch to activate it.

2 Drag the adjustment bar to adjust the filter's opacity.

3 To set the schedule to apply the blue light filter to the screen, tap the **Turn on as scheduled** switch to activate it and select an option.

- **Sunset to sunrise**: Set the device to apply the blue light filter at night and turn it off in the morning based on your current location.
- **Custom schedule**: Set a specific time to apply the blue light filter.

Changing the screen mode or adjusting the display colour

Select a screen mode suitable for viewing movies or images, or adjust the display colour to your preference. If you select the **Adaptive display** mode, you can adjust the display colour balance by colour value.

Changing the screen mode

On the Settings screen, tap **Display** → **Screen mode** and select a mode you want.

- **Adaptive display**: This optimises the colour range, saturation, and sharpness of your display. You can also adjust the display colour balance by colour value.
- **AMOLED cinema**: This is suitable for watching videos.
- **AMOLED photo**: This is suitable for viewing images.
- **Basic**: This is set as default and is suitable for general use.

> - You can adjust the display colour only in **Adaptive display** mode.
> - **Adaptive display** mode may not be compatible with third-party apps.
> - You cannot change the screen mode while applying the blue light filter.

Settings

Optimising the full screen colour balance

Optimise the display colour by adjusting the colour tones to your preference.

When you drag the colour adjustment bar towards **Cool**, the blue colour tone will increase. When you drag the bar towards **Warm**, the red colour tone will increase.

1 On the Settings screen, tap **Display** → **Screen mode** → **Adaptive display**.

2 Tap .

3 Adjust the colour adjustment bar under **Full screen colour balance**.

The colour balance of the screen will be optimised.

Adjusting the screen tone by colour value

Increase or lower certain colour tones by adjusting the **Red**, **Green**, or **Blue** value individually.

1 On the Settings screen, tap **Display** → **Screen mode** → **Adaptive display**.

2 Tap .

3 Tick **Advanced options**.

4 Adjust the **Red**, **Green**, or **Blue** colour bar to your preference.

The screen tone screen will be adjusted.

Settings

Screen resolution

Change the screen resolution. It is set to FHD+ by default. Higher resolutions make the display more vivid, however they will consume more battery power.

1 On the Settings screen, tap **Display** → **Screen resolution**.

2 Select a resolution option and tap **Apply**.

Some currently running apps may close when you change the resolution.

Screensaver

You can set to display images as a screensaver when the screen turns off automatically. The screensaver will be displayed when the device is charging.

1 On the Settings screen, tap **Display** → **Screensaver** and tap the switch to activate it.

2 Select an option.

If you select **Photo Frame**, a slideshow with selected images will start. If you select **Photo Table** or **Photos**, selected images will appear as small cards and overlap.

3 Tap ✱ to select albums for displaying images.

4 When you are finished, tap the Back button.

To preview the selected option, tap **Preview**.

When you tap the screen while your screensaver is displayed, the screen will turn on.

Settings

Wallpapers and themes

Change the wallpaper settings for the Home screen and the locked screen or apply various themes to the device.

On the Settings screen, tap **Wallpapers and themes**.

- **Wallpapers**: Change the wallpaper settings for the Home screen and the locked screen.
- **Themes**: Change the device's theme.
- **Icons**: Change the icon style.
- **AODs**: Select an image to display on the Always On Display.

Lock screen

Options

Change the settings for the locked screen.

On the Settings screen, tap **Lock screen**.

The available options may vary depending on the screen lock method selected.

- **Screen lock type**: Change the screen lock method.
- **Smart Lock**: Set the device to unlock itself when trusted locations or devices are detected. Refer to Smart Lock for more information.
- **Secure lock settings**: Change screen lock settings for the selected lock method.
- **Always On Display**: Set the device to display information while the screen is turned off. Refer to Always On Display for more information.
- **Clock style**: Change the type and colour of the clock on the locked screen.
- **Roaming clock**: Change the clock to show both the local and home time zones on the locked screen when roaming.

Settings

- **FaceWidgets**: Change the settings of the items displayed on the locked screen.
- **Contact information**: Set the device to show contact information, such as your email address, on the locked screen.
- **Notifications**: Set how to show notifications on the locked screen.
- **App shortcuts**: Select apps to display shortcuts to them on the locked screen.
- **About Lock screen**: View the Locked screen version and legal information.

Smart Lock

You can set the device to unlock itself and remain unlocked when trusted locations or devices are detected.

For example, if you have set your home as a trusted location, when you get home your device will detect the location and automatically unlock itself.

- This feature will be available to use after you set a screen lock method.
- If you do not use your device for four hours or when you turn on the device, you must unlock the screen using the pattern, PIN, or password you set.

1 On the Settings screen, tap **Lock screen** → **Smart Lock**.
2 Unlock the screen using the preset screen lock method.
3 Select an option and follow the on-screen instructions to complete the setting.

Settings

Biometrics and security

Options

Change the settings for securing the device.

On the Settings screen, tap **Biometrics and security**.

- **Intelligent Scan**: Register both your face and irises to the device to unlock the screen more conveniently. Refer to Intelligent Scan for more information.
- **Face recognition**: Set the device to unlock the screen by recognising your face. Refer to Face recognition for more information.
- **Irises**: Register your irises to unlock the screen. Refer to Iris recognition for more information.
- **Fingerprints**: Register your fingerprints to unlock the screen. Refer to Fingerprint recognition for more information.
- **Biometrics preferences**: Change the settings for biometric data.
- **Google Play Protect**: Set the device to check for harmful apps and behaviour and warn about potential harm and remove them.
- **Find My Mobile**: Activate or deactivate the Find My Mobile feature. Access the Find My Mobile website (findmymobile.samsung.com) to track and control your lost or stolen device.

  You can also allow the Google location service to provide more accurate information about the location of your device.
- **Security update**: View the version of your device's software and check for updates.
- **Samsung Pass**: Verify your identity easily and securely via your biometric data. Refer to Samsung Pass for more information.
- **Install unknown apps**: Set the device to allow the installation of apps from unknown sources.

Settings

- **Secure Folder**: Create a secure folder to protect your private content and apps from others. Refer to Secure Folder for more information.
- **Secure startup**: Protect your device by setting it to require a screen unlock code when turning on the device. You must enter the unlock code to start the device and receive messages and notifications.
- **Encrypt SD card**: Set the device to encrypt files on a memory card.

> If you reset your device to the factory defaults with this setting enabled, the device will not be able to read your encrypted files. Disable this setting before resetting the device.

- **Other security settings**: Configure additional security settings.
- **Location**: Change settings for location information permissions.
- **App permissions**: View the list of features and apps that have permission to use them. You can also edit the permission settings.
- **App permission monitor**: Set to receive notifications when the permissions you select are used by apps that you are not using. You can manage the settings of each app.
- **Report diagnostic info to Samsung**: Set the device to automatically send the device's diagnostic and usage information to Samsung.
- **Receiving marketing information**: Set whether to receive Samsung marketing information, such as special offers, membership benefits, and newsletters.

Settings

Intelligent Scan

By using both your face and irises, you can easily and conveniently unlock the screen and verify your identity.

- This feature may not be available depending on the region or service provider.
- If you use Intelligent Scan as a screen lock method, your face and irises cannot be used to unlock the screen for the first time after turning on the device. To use the device, you must unlock the screen using the pattern, PIN, or password you set when registering your face and irises. Be careful not to forget your pattern, PIN, or password.
- If your irises are not recognised, unlock the device using the pattern, PIN, or password you set when registering the irises, and then re-register your irises. If your pattern, PIN, or password is forgotten, you will not be able to use the device if you do not reset it. Samsung is not responsible for any data loss or inconvenience caused by forgotten unlock codes.
- If you change the screen lock method to **Swipe** or **None**, which are not secure, all of your biometric data will be deleted. If you want to use your biometric data in apps or features, you must register your biometric data again.

Precautions for using Intelligent Scan

Before using Intelligent Scan, keep the following precautions in mind.

- To protect your eyes, keep the screen at least 20 cm away from your face when using iris recognition.
- If you attach screen protectors (privacy protection films, tempered glass protectors, etc.), the recognition may fail.
- Do not use this feature with infants. Doing so may damage their eyesight.

Settings

- Anyone who has experienced dizziness, seizures, loss of awareness, blackouts, or other symptoms linked to an epileptic condition, or has a family history of such symptoms or conditions, should consult a doctor before using this feature.
- Intelligent Scan is not intended for any diagnostic, therapeutic, or preventative medical purposes.
- Your phone could be unlocked by someone that looks like you.
- Keep secure of your phone and do not let anyone else unlock your phone.

For better face and iris recognition

The phone may not recognise your irises or face when:
- something prevents a good view of your face or eyes (e.g. glasses, contact lenses, hat, low eyelids, recent eye surgery, disease, dirt, damage to the camera, or excessive movement).

Registering irises and face

1 On the Settings screen, tap **Biometrics and security** → **Intelligent Scan**.

2 Unlock the screen using the preset screen lock method.
   If you have not set a screen lock method, create one.

3 Read the on-screen instructions and tap **Continue**.

4 Select whether you are wearing glasses or not and tap **Continue**.

5 Register your face and irises.
   For more information, refer to Face recognition and Iris recognition.

Settings

Deleting registered face and iris data

You can delete face and iris data that you have registered.

1 On the Settings screen, tap **Biometrics and security** → **Intelligent Scan**.

2 Unlock the screen using the preset screen lock method.

3 Tap **Remove face and iris data** → **Remove**.

Once the registered face and iris data has been deleted, all the related features will also be deactivated.

Unlocking the screen using Intelligent Scan

You can unlock the screen with your face and irises instead of using a pattern, PIN, or password.

1 On the Settings screen, tap **Biometrics and security** → **Intelligent Scan**.

2 Unlock the screen using the preset screen lock method.

3 Tap the **Intelligent Scan unlock** switch to activate it.

4 On the locked screen, look at the screen.

When your face and irises are recognised, you can unlock the screen without using any additional screen lock method. If your face and irises are not recognised, use the preset screen lock method.

Settings

Face recognition

You can set the device to unlock the screen by recognising your face.

- If you use your face as a screen lock method, your face cannot be used to unlock the screen for the first time after turning on the device. To use the device, you must unlock the screen using the pattern, PIN, or password you set when registering the face. Be careful not to forget your pattern, PIN, or password.
- If you change the screen lock method to **Swipe** or **None**, which are not secure, all of your biometric data will be deleted. If you want to use your biometric data in apps or features, you must register your biometric data again.

Precautions for using face recognition

Before using the face recognition to unlock your device, keep the following precautions in mind.

- Your device could be unlocked by someone or something that looks like your image.
- Face recognition is less secure than Pattern, PIN, or Password.

For better face recognition

Consider the following when using face recognition:

- Consider the conditions when registering, such as wearing glasses, hats, masks, beards, or heavy makeup
- Ensure that you are in a well-lit area and that the camera lens is clean when registering
- Ensure your image is not blurry for better match results

Settings

Registering your face

For better face registration, register your face indoors and out of direct sunlight.

1 On the Settings screen, tap **Biometrics and security** → **Face recognition**.

2 Unlock the screen using the preset screen lock method.
If you have not set a screen lock method, create one.

3 Read the on-screen instructions and tap **Continue**.

4 Select whether you are wearing glasses or not and tap **Continue**.

5 Hold the device with the screen facing towards you and look at the screen.

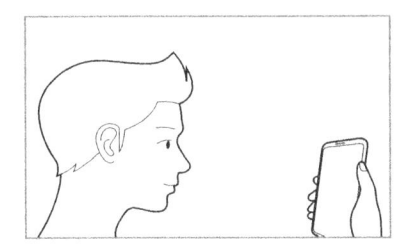

6 Position your face inside the frame on the screen.
The camera will scan your face.
When the useful face recognition screen appears, turn on a switch to activate a feature and tap **OK**.

If unlocking the screen with your face is not working properly, tap **Remove face data** to remove your registered face and register your face again.

Settings

Deleting the registered face data

You can delete face data that you have registered.

1 On the Settings screen, tap **Biometrics and security** → **Face recognition**.

2 Unlock the screen using the preset screen lock method.

3 Tap **Remove face data** → **Remove**.

Once the registered face is deleted, all the related features will also be deactivated.

Unlocking the screen with your face

You can unlock the screen with your face instead of using a pattern, PIN, or password.

1 On the Settings screen, tap **Biometrics and security** → **Face recognition**.

2 Unlock the screen using the preset screen lock method.

3 Tap the **Face unlock** switch to activate it.

If you want to reduce the possibility of recognising faces in photos or videos, tap the **Faster recognition** switch to deactivate it. This may decrease the face recognition speed.

4 On the locked screen, look at the screen.

When your face is recognised, you can unlock the screen without using any additional screen lock method. If your face is not recognised, use the preset screen lock method.

Settings

Iris recognition

The iris recognition feature uses the unique characteristics of your irises, such as their shape and pattern, to strengthen the security of your device. Your iris data can be used for various authentication purposes. After registering your irises, you can set the device to use your irises for the following features:

- Samsung Pass (Samsung account verification and web sign-in)
- Samsung Pay
- Screen lock
- Secure Folder

- This feature may not be available depending on the region or service provider.
- If you use your iris as a screen lock method, your irises cannot be used to unlock the screen for the first time after turning on the device. To use the device, you must unlock the screen using the pattern, PIN, or password you set when registering the irises. Be careful not to forget your pattern, PIN, or password.
- If your irises are not recognised, unlock the device using the pattern, PIN, or password you set when registering the irises, and then re-register your irises. If your pattern, PIN, or password is forgotten, you will not be able to use the device if you do not reset it. Samsung is not responsible for any data loss or inconvenience caused by forgotten unlock codes.
- If you change the screen lock method to **Swipe** or **None**, which are not secure, all of your biometric data will be deleted. If you want to use your biometric data in apps or features, you must register your biometric data again.

Settings

⚠ Precautions for using iris recognition

Before using iris recognition, keep the following precautions in mind.

- To protect your eyes, keep the screen at least 20 cm away from your face when using iris recognition.
- If you attach screen protectors (privacy protection films, tempered glass protectors, etc.), the recognition may fail.
- Do not use iris recognition with infants. Doing so may damage their eyesight.
- Anyone who has experienced dizziness, seizures, loss of awareness, blackouts, or other symptoms linked to an epileptic condition, or has a family history of such symptoms or conditions, should consult a doctor before using iris recognition.
- Biometric data collected and stored locally by the iris scanner is not intended for any diagnostic, therapeutic, or preventative medical purposes.

For better iris recognition

The phone may not recognise your eyes when:

- something prevents the camera from getting a good view of your irises (e.g. glasses, low eyelids, recent eye surgery, disease, dirt, damage to the camera, or excessive movement).
- the lighting is very different from when you recorded your irises (e.g. direct sunlight).

Hold your device about 25-35 cm away from your face with the screen facing towards you.

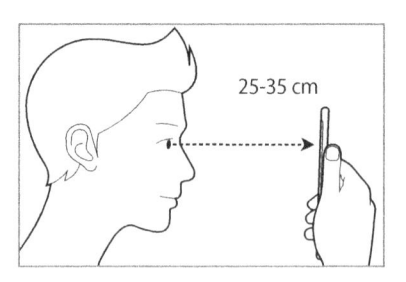

Settings

Registering irises

The device can save the iris data of one person only. You cannot register more than one set of irises.

1 On the Settings screen, tap **Biometrics and security** → **Irises**.

2 Unlock the screen using the preset screen lock method.
   If you have not set a screen lock method, create one.

3 Read the on-screen instructions and tap **Continue** → **Continue**.
   To register only one iris of your eyes, tick **Register just 1 iris**.

4 Hold the device with the screen facing towards you and look at the screen.

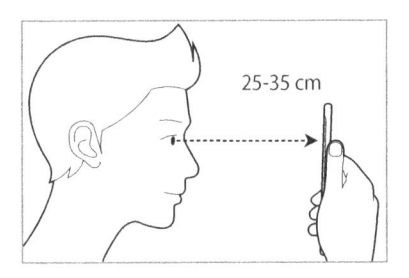

25-35 cm

5 Position your eyes inside the circles on the screen and open your eyes wide.
   The iris recognition camera will scan your irises.

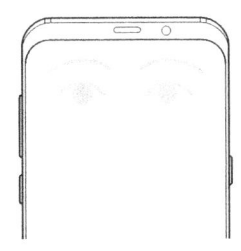

Settings

Deleting registered iris data

You can delete iris data that you have registered.

1 On the Settings screen, tap **Biometrics and security** → **Irises**.

2 Unlock the screen using the preset screen lock method.

3 Tap **Remove iris data** → **REMOVE**.

Once the registered iris data has been deleted, all the related features will also be deactivated.

Using Samsung Pass

When you register your irises to Samsung Pass, you can use them to easily verify your identity or sign in to websites. Refer to Samsung Pass for more information.

Using irises with Samsung Pay

You can use irises with Samsung Pay to make payments quickly and securely. Refer to Samsung Pay for more information.

Samsung Pay may not be available depending on the region or service provider.

Settings

Unlocking the screen with your irises

You can unlock the screen with your irises instead of using a pattern, PIN, or password.

1 On the Settings screen, tap **Biometrics and security** → **Irises**.

2 Unlock the screen using the preset screen lock method.

3 Tap the **Iris unlock** switch to activate it.

4 On the locked screen, swipe in any direction and position your eyes inside the circles on the screen to scan your irises.

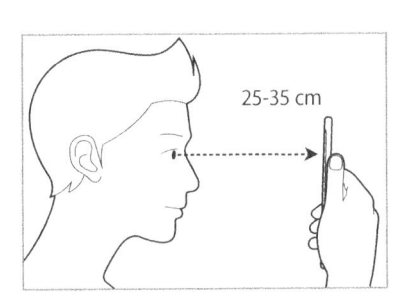

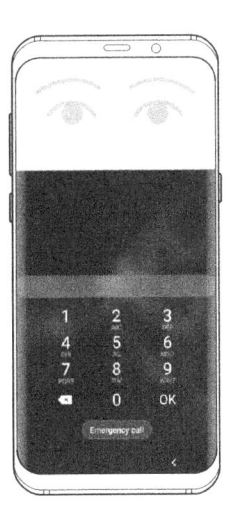

To unlock the screen using iris recognition, without swiping on the locked screen, tap **Screen-on iris recognition** switch to activate it.

Settings

Fingerprint recognition

In order for fingerprint recognition to function, your fingerprint information needs to be registered and stored in your device. After registering, you can set the device to use your fingerprint for the features below:

- Samsung Pass (Samsung account verification and web sign-in)
- Samsung Pay
- Screen lock
- Secure Folder

- This feature may not be available depending on the region or service provider.
- Fingerprint recognition uses the unique characteristics of each fingerprint to enhance the security of your device. The likelihood of the fingerprint sensor confusing two different fingerprints is very low. However, in rare cases where separate fingerprints are very similar the sensor may recognise them as identical.
- If you use your fingerprint as a screen lock method, your fingerprint cannot be used to unlock the screen for the first time after turning on the device. To use the device, you must unlock the screen using the pattern, PIN, or password you set when registering the fingerprint. Be careful not to forget your pattern, PIN, or password.
- If your fingerprint is not recognised, unlock the device using the pattern, PIN, or password you set when registering the fingerprint, and then re-register your fingerprints. If your pattern, PIN, or password is forgotten, you will not be able to use the device if you do not reset it. Samsung is not responsible for any data loss or inconvenience caused by forgotten unlock codes.
- If you change the screen lock method to **Swipe** or **None**, which are not secure, all of your biometric data will be deleted. If you want to use your biometric data in apps or features, you must register your biometric data again.

Settings

For better fingerprint recognition

When you scan your fingerprints on the device, be aware of the following conditions that may affect the feature's performance:

- The fingerprint recognition sensor recognises fingerprints. Ensure that the fingerprint recognition sensor is not scratched or damaged by metal objects, such as coins, keys, and necklaces.
- Covering the fingerprint recognition sensor with protective films, stickers, or other accessories may decrease the fingerprint recognition rate. If the fingerprint recognition sensor is initially covered with a protective film, remove it before using the fingerprint recognition sensor.
- Ensure that the fingerprint recognition sensor and your fingers are clean and dry.
- The device may not recognise fingerprints that are affected by wrinkles or scars.
- The device may not recognise fingerprints from small or thin fingers.
- If you bend your finger or use a fingertip, the device may not recognise your fingerprints. Make sure to cover the entire fingerprint recognition sensor with your finger.
- To improve recognition performance, register fingerprints of the hand used most often to perform tasks on the device.
- In dry environments, static electricity can build up in the device. Avoid using this feature in dry environments or before using the feature, discharge static electricity by touching a metal object.

Registering fingerprints

1 On the Settings screen, tap **Biometrics and security** → **Fingerprints**.

2 Unlock the screen using the preset screen lock method.

If you have not set a screen lock method, create one.

Settings

3 Swipe your finger downwards over the fingerprint recognition sensor.

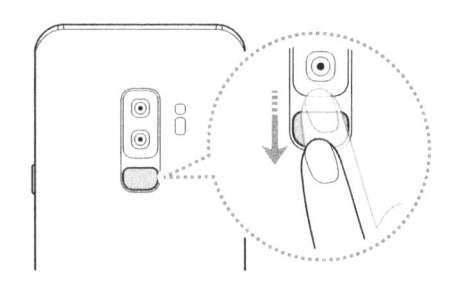

Repeat this action until the fingerprint is registered. When you are finished registering your fingerprints, tap **Done**.

Deleting registered fingerprints

You can delete registered fingerprints.

1 On the Settings screen, tap **Biometrics and security** → **Fingerprints**.

2 Unlock the screen using the preset screen lock method.

3 Select a fingerprint to delete and tap **Remove** → **Remove**.

Using Samsung Pass

When you register your fingerprints to Samsung Pass, you can use them to easily verify your identity or sign in to websites. Refer to Samsung Pass for more information.

Using fingerprints with Samsung Pay

You can use fingerprints with Samsung Pay to make payments quickly and securely. Refer to Samsung Pay for more information.

Samsung Pay may not be available depending on the region or service provider.

Settings

Unlocking the screen with your fingerprints

You can unlock the screen with your fingerprint instead of using a pattern, PIN, or password.

1 On the Settings screen, tap **Biometrics and security** → **Fingerprints**.

2 Unlock the screen using the preset screen lock method.

3 Tap the **Fingerprint unlock** switch to activate it.

4 On the locked screen, place your finger on the fingerprint recognition sensor and scan your fingerprint.

Samsung Pass

Samsung Pass allows you to sign in to your Samsung account, websites, or apps more easily and securely via your biometric data, such as fingerprints or irises, rather than entering your login information. Also, Samsung Pass allows you to enter the personal information, such as your address or payment card information, more easily and quickly via your registered biometric data.

Register your biometric data to Samsung Pass and set to sign in to supported websites or apps using the data via Samsung Pass.

- To use this feature, your device must be connected to a Wi-Fi or mobile network.
- To use this feature, you must register and sign in to your Samsung account. For more information, refer to Samsung account.
- The website sign-in feature is only available for websites that you access via the **Internet** app. Some websites may not support this feature.
- Registered biometric data and saved payment card information are only saved to your device and are not synced with other devices or servers.

Settings

Registering Samsung Pass

Before using Samsung Pass, register your biometric data to Samsung Pass.

1 On the Settings screen, tap **Biometrics and security** → **Samsung Pass**.

2 Read the on-screen instructions and tap **Continue** → **Sign-in**.

3 Enter your Samsung account ID and password and tap **Sign in**.

4 Agree to the terms and conditions of Samsung Pass.

5 Tap **Fingerprints** or **Irises** and register your fingerprints or irises.

Refer to Fingerprint recognition or Iris recognition for more information.

6 Scan your fingerprint or irises and tap **Next** to complete the Samsung Pass registration.

If the **Add Samsung Pass to Home screen** option is ticked, the Samsung Pass icon will be added on the Home screen.

If the **Use Samsung Pass instead of Samsung account password** option is ticked, you can use your registered biometric data to verify your identity instead of entering the Samsung account password.

Verifying the Samsung account password

You can use your registered biometric data to verify your identity instead of entering your Samsung account password when, for example, you purchase content from **Galaxy Apps**.

1 On the Settings screen, tap **Biometrics and security** → **Samsung Pass**.

2 Unlock the screen using the preset screen lock method.

3 Tap ⋮ → **Settings** → **Samsung account**, and then tap the **Verify with Samsung Pass** switch to activate it.

Settings

Using Samsung Pass to sign in to websites

You can use Samsung Pass to easily sign in to websites that support ID and password autofill.

1 Open a website that you want to sign in to.

2 Enter your user name and password, and then tap the website's sign in button.

3 When a pop-up window asking whether you want to save the sign-in information appears, tick **Sign in with Samsung Pass** and tap **Remember**.

You can now use the biometric data you registered to Samsung Pass when signing in to the website.

Using Samsung Pass to sign in to apps

You can use Samsung Pass to easily sign in to apps that support ID and password autofill.

1 Open an app that you want to sign in to.

2 Enter your user name and password, and then tap the app's sign in button.

3 When a pop-up window asking whether you want to save the sign-in information appears, tap **Save**.

You can now use the biometric data you registered to Samsung Pass when signing in to the app.

Settings

Managing sign-in information

View the list of websites and apps you have set to use Samsung Pass and manage your sign-in information.

1 On the Settings screen, tap **Biometrics and security** → **Samsung Pass**.

2 Unlock the screen using the preset screen lock method.

3 Tap **Sign-in** and select a website or app from the list.

4 Tap ⋮ → **Edit** and modify your ID, password, and the website's or app's name.
To delete the website or app, tap ⋮ → **Delete**.

Using Samsung Pass with websites and apps

When using websites or apps that support Samsung Pass, you can easily sign in with Samsung Pass.

To see the list of websites and apps that support Samsung Pass, on the Settings screen, tap **Biometrics and security** → **Samsung Pass**, unlock the screen using your preset screen lock method, and then tap ⋮ → **Partners**. If there are no websites or apps that support Samsung Pass, **Partners** will not appear.

- Available websites and apps may vary depending on the region or service provider.
- Samsung is not responsible for any loss or inconvenience caused by signing in to websites or apps via Samsung Pass.

Settings

Entering your personal information automatically

You can use Samsung Pass to easily enter your address or payment card information on apps that support autofilling personal information.

1 On the Settings screen, tap **Biometrics and security** → **Samsung Pass**.

2 Unlock the screen using the preset screen lock method.

3 Tap **Autofill forms** and select **Add address** or **Add card**.

4 Enter the information and tap **Save**.

You can now use the biometric data you registered to Samsung Pass when entering the personal information automatically on supported apps.

Deleting your Samsung Pass data

You can delete your biometric data, sign-in information, and app data registered to Samsung Pass. Your agreement to the terms and conditions and your Samsung account will remain active.

1 On the Settings screen, tap **Biometrics and security** → **Samsung Pass**.

2 Unlock the screen using the preset screen lock method.

3 Tap ⋮ → **Settings** → **Delete data** → **Delete**.

4 Enter your Samsung account password and tap **OK**.

Your Samsung Pass data will be deleted.

Settings

Secure Folder

Secure Folder protects your private content and apps, such as photos and contacts, from being accessed by others. You can keep your private content and apps secure even when the device is unlocked.

Secure Folder is a separate, secured storage area. The data in Secure Folder cannot be transferred to other devices via unapproved sharing methods, such as USB or Wi-Fi Direct. Attempting to customise the operating system or modifying software will cause Secure Folder to be automatically locked and inaccessible. Before saving data in Secure Folder, make sure to back up a copy of the data in another secure location.

Settings

Setting up Secure Folder

1. Launch the **Settings** app and tap **Biometrics and security** → **Secure Folder**.

2. Tap **Continue**.

3. Enter your Samsung account ID and password and tap **Sign in**.

4. Read and agree to the terms and conditions and tap **Next**.

5. Select a lock method to use for Secure Folder and follow the on-screen instructions to complete the setup.
   To change the name or icon colour of Secure Folder, tap ⁝ → **Customise icon**.

- When you launch the **Secure Folder** app, you must unlock the app using your preset lock method.
- If you forget your Secure Folder unlock code, you can reset it using your Samsung account. Tap the reset button at the bottom of the locked screen, and enter your Samsung account password.

Setting auto lock for Secure Folder

Set the device to automatically lock Secure Folder when it is not being used.

1. Launch the **Secure Folder** app and tap ⁝ → **Settings** → **Auto lock Secure Folder**.

2. Select a lock option.

To manually lock your Secure Folder, tap ⁝ → **Lock**.

Settings

Moving content to Secure Folder

Move content, such as photos and contacts, to Secure Folder. The following actions are an example of moving an image from the default storage to Secure Folder.

1 Launch the **Secure Folder** app and tap **Add files**.

2 Tap **Images**, tick images to move, and then tap **Done**.

3 Tap **Move**.
 The selected items will be deleted from the original folder and moved to Secure Folder. To copy items, tap **Copy**.

 The method for moving content may vary depending on the content type.

Moving content from Secure Folder

Move content from Secure Folder to the corresponding app in the default storage. The following actions are an example of moving an image from Secure Folder to the default storage.

1 Launch the **Secure Folder** app and tap **Gallery**.

2 Select an image and tap ⋮ → **Move out of Secure Folder**.
 The selected items will be moved to **Gallery** in the default storage.

Settings

Adding apps

Add an app to use in Secure Folder.

1 Launch the **Secure Folder** app and tap **Add apps**.

2 Tick one or more apps installed on the device and tap **Add**.

To install apps from **Play Store** or **Galaxy Apps**, tap **Download from Play Store** or **Download from Galaxy Store**.

Removing apps from Secure Folder

Tap and hold an app to delete, and tap **Uninstall**.

Adding accounts

Add your Samsung and Google accounts, or other accounts, to sync with the apps in Secure Folder.

1 Launch the **Secure Folder** app and tap → **Settings** → **Accounts** → **Add account**.

2 Select an account service.

3 Follow the on-screen instructions to complete the account setup.

Hiding Secure Folder

You can hide the Secure Folder shortcut from the Apps screen.

Launch the **Secure Folder** app, tap → **Settings**, and then tap the **Show Secure Folder** switch to deactivate it.

Alternatively, drag the status bar downwards to open the notification panel. Then, swipe downwards on the notification panel and tap **Secure Folder** to deactivate the feature.

Settings

Backing up and restoring Secure Folder

Back up content and apps in Secure Folder to Samsung Cloud using your Samsung account and restore them later.

Backing up data

1. Launch the **Secure Folder** app and tap → **Settings** → **Backup and restore**.
2. Tap **Add account** and sign in to your Samsung account.
3. Tap **Back up Secure Folder data**.
4. Tick items you want to back up and tap **Back up now**.
   Data will be backed up to Samsung Cloud.

Restoring data

1. Launch the **Secure Folder** app and tap → **Settings** → **Backup and restore**.
2. Tap **Restore**.
3. Tap ▼ to select a device to restore the data.
4. Select the data types you want to restore and tap **Restore now**.
   Backed up data will be restored to your device.

Uninstalling Secure Folder

You can uninstall Secure Folder, including the content and apps in it.

Launch the **Secure Folder** app and tap → **Settings** → **More settings** → **Uninstall**.

To back up content before uninstalling Secure Folder, tick **Move media files out of Secure Folder** and tap **UNINSTALL**. To access data backed from Secure Folder, open the **Samsung** folder, launch the **My Files** app, and then tap **Internal storage** → **Secure Folder**.

Notes saved in **Samsung Notes** will not be backed up.

Settings

Accounts and backup

Options

Sync, back up, or restore your device's data using Samsung Cloud. You can also register and manage accounts, such as your Samsung account or Google account, or transfer data to or from other devices via Smart Switch.

On the Settings screen, tap **Accounts and backup**.

- **Accounts**: Add your Samsung and Google accounts, or other accounts, to sync with.
- **Backup and restore**: Keep your personal information, app data, and settings safe on your device. You can back up your sensitive information and access it later. You must sign in to your Google or Samsung account to back up or restore data.
- **Samsung Cloud**: Manage the content that you want to store securely in Samsung Cloud. Check the usage status of your Samsung Cloud storage, and sync, back up, and restore your data. Refer to Samsung Cloud for more information.
- **Smart Switch**: Launch Smart Switch and transfer data from your previous device. Refer to Transferring data from your previous device (Smart Switch) for more information.

Regularly back up your data to a safe location, such as Samsung Cloud or a computer, so that you can restore it if the data is corrupted or lost due to an unintended factory data reset.

Settings

Samsung Cloud

Back up data from your previous device to Samsung Cloud and restore the data to your new device. You can also sync data saved in your device with Samsung Cloud and view data saved on the Samsung Cloud. You must register and sign in to your Samsung account to use Samsung Cloud. Refer to Samsung account for more information.

Backing up data from your previous device

1 On your previous device, sign in to your Samsung account.

2 Launch the **Settings** app, select the backup option, and back up your data.

- If your device supports Samsung Cloud, launch the **Settings** app, tap **Accounts and backup** → **Samsung Cloud** → **Back up this phone**, tick items you want to back up, and then tap **Back up** to back up your data.
- The data backup method may vary depending on your model.
- Some data will not be backed up. To check which data will be backed up, launch the **Settings** app, tap **Accounts and backup** → **Samsung Cloud** → **Back up this phone**.
- To view the backup data for each device in your Samsung Cloud, launch the **Settings** app, tap **Accounts and backup** → **Samsung Cloud** → **Restore data** → ▼, and then select a device you want.

Restoring data from your previous device

1 On your new device, launch the **Settings** app and tap **Accounts and backup** → **Samsung Cloud**.

2 Tap **Restore data** → ▼ and select a previous device.

3 Tick the data types you want to restore and tap **Restore**.

Syncing data from your device

You can sync data saved in your device, such as images, videos, and events, with Samsung Cloud and access it from other devices.

1 On your new device, launch the **Settings** app and tap **Accounts and backup** → **Samsung Cloud**.

2 Tap ⋮ → **Settings** → **Sync and auto backup settings** → **Sync**.

3 Tap the switches next to the items you want to sync with.

You can check the saved data or change the settings by tapping the **Gallery**, **Other synced data**, or **Samsung Cloud Drive**.

Google

Configure settings for some features provided by Google.

On the Settings screen, tap **Google**.

Settings

Advanced features

Options

Activate advanced features and change the settings that control them.

On the Settings screen, tap **Advanced features**.

> Excessive shaking or an impact to the device may cause an unintended input for some features using sensors.

- **Smart pop-up view**: Select apps to view their notifications via pop-up windows. When using this feature, you can quickly view the contents via pop-up windows by tapping the icon on the screen.

    > This feature is only available in apps that support the Multi window feature.

- **Smart capture**: Set the device to capture the current screen and scrollable area, and crop and share the screenshot immediately.
- **Direct share**: Set the device to display the people you contacted on the sharing options panel to allow you to share content directly.
- **Reduce animations**: Set the device to reduce certain screen effects if you are sensitive to animations or screen movement.
- **Motions and gestures**: Activate the motion feature and configure settings.
- **Game Launcher**: Activate the Game Launcher. Refer to Game Launcher for more information.
- **Dual Messenger**: Install the second app and use two separate accounts for the same messenger app. Refer to Dual Messenger for more information.
- **Video enhancer**: Enhance the image quality of your videos to enjoy brighter and more vivid colours.

    > This feature may not be available in some apps.

- **Send SOS messages**: Set the device to send help messages by pressing the Power key three times. You can also send sound recordings along with the message to the recipients.

Settings

Dual Messenger

Install the second app and use two separate accounts for the same messenger app.

1 On the Settings screen, tap **Advanced features** → **Dual Messenger**.

   Supported apps will appear.

2 Tap the switch of an app to install the second app.

   The second app will be installed. The second app's icon will be displayed with . When you receive notifications from the second app, the notifications will be displayed with to distinguish them from the first app's notifications.

Second app

- The Dual Messenger feature may not be available depending on the app.
- Some features of the app may be limited for the second app.

Uninstalling a second app

1 On the Settings screen, tap **Advanced features** → **Dual Messenger**.

2 Tap the switch of the app you want to disable and tap **Disable** or **Uninstall**.

   All data related to the second app will be deleted.

If you uninstall the first app, the second app will also be deleted.

Settings

Device care

The device care feature provides an overview of the status of your device's battery, storage, memory, and system security. You can also automatically optimise the device with a tap of your finger.

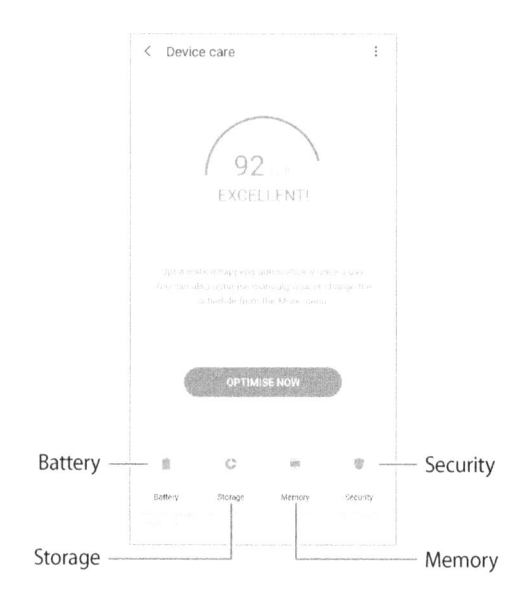

Battery — Security

Storage — Memory

Using the quick optimisation feature

On the Settings screen, tap **Device care** → **FIX NOW** or **OPTIMISE NOW**.

The quick optimisation feature improves device performance through the following actions.

- Clearing some memory.
- Deleting unnecessary files and closing apps running in the background.
- Managing abnormal battery usage.
- Scanning for crashed apps and malware.

238

Settings

Battery

Check the remaining battery power and time to use the device. For devices with low battery levels, conserve battery power by activating power saving features.

On the Settings screen, tap **Device care** → **Battery**.

- The usage time left shows the time remaining before the battery power runs out. Usage time left may vary depending on your device settings and operating conditions.
- You may not receive notifications from some apps that use power saving mode.

Managing battery usage

Select a power mode that suits your device usage purposes.

Tap **Power mode** and select an option.

- **High performance**: The screen is as bright as possible and at maximum resolution. The battery may drain quickly.
- **Optimised**: Optimised for a balance between the device's performance and battery usage.
- **Medium power saving**: Activate power saving mode to extend the battery's usage time.
- **Maximum power saving**: In maximum power saving mode, the device decreases battery consumption by activating night mode and limiting the apps and features available. Network connections, except for the mobile network, will be deactivated.

You can set the device to charge the battery more quickly. Tap ⋮ → **Settings** and tap the **Fast cable charging** switch to activate it.

Managing battery usage for each app

You can save battery power by preventing apps that are running in the background from using battery power when they are not being used. Select apps from the apps list and tap the **Put app to sleep** switch to activate the feature. Also, tap ⋮ → **Settings** and set up the options under **App power management**.

Settings

Storage

Check the status of the used and available memory.

On the Settings screen, tap **Device care** → **Storage**.

- The actual available capacity of the internal memory is less than the specified capacity because the operating system and default apps occupy part of the memory. The available capacity may change when you update the device.
- You can view the available capacity of the internal memory in the Specification section for your device on the Samsung website.

Managing the memory

To delete residual files, such as cache, tap **CLEAN NOW**. To delete files or uninstall apps that you do not use any more, select a category under **App data** or **User data**. Then, tick items to select and tap **DELETE** or **UNINSTALL**.

Memory

On the Settings screen, tap **Device care** → **Memory**.

To speed up your device by stopping apps running in the background, tick apps from the apps list, and tap **CLEAN NOW**.

Security

Check the device's security status. This feature scans your device for malware.

On the Settings screen, tap **Device care** → **Security** → **SCAN PHONE**.

Apps

Manage the device's apps and change their settings. You can view the apps' usage information, change their notification or permission settings, or uninstall or disable unnecessary apps.

On the Settings screen, tap **Apps**.

Settings

General management

Customise your device's system settings or reset the device.

On the Settings screen, tap **General management**.

- **Language and input**: Select device languages and change settings, such as keyboards and voice input types. Some options may not be available depending on the selected language. Refer to Adding device languages for more information.
- **Date and time**: Access and alter the settings to control how the device displays the time and date.

  If the battery remains fully discharged, the time and date is reset.

- **Contact us**: Ask questions or view frequently asked questions. Refer to Samsung Members for more information.
- **Reset**: Reset your device's settings or perform a factory data reset. You can reset all your settings, or only network settings, or accessibility settings. You can also set the device to restart at a preset time for device optimisation.

Adding device languages

You can add languages to use on your device.

1. On the Settings screen, tap **General management** → **Language and input** → **Language** → **Add language**.

   To view all the languages that can be added, tap ⋮ → **All languages**.

2. Select a language to add.

3. To set the selected language as the default language, tap **Set as default**. To keep the current language setting, tap **Keep current**.

   The selected language will be added to your languages list. If you changed the default language, the selected language will be added to the top of the list.

To change the default language from your languages list, drag ◌ next to a language and move it to the top of the list. Then, tap **Apply**. If an app does not support the default language, the next supported language in the list will be used.

Settings

Accessibility

Configure various settings to improve accessibility to the device. Refer to Accessibility for more information.

On the Settings screen, tap **Accessibility**.

Software update

Update your device's software via the firmware over-the-air (FOTA) service. You can also schedule software updates.

On the Settings screen, tap **Software update**.

If emergency software updates are released for your device's security and to block new types of security threats, they will be installed automatically without your agreement.

- **Download and install**: Check for and install updates manually.
- **Auto download over Wi-Fi**: Set the device to download updates automatically when connected to a Wi-Fi network.
- **Last update**: View information about the last software update.

Security updates information

Security updates are provided to strengthen the security of your device and protect your personal information. For security updates for your model, visit security.samsungmobile.com.

The website supports only some languages.

Settings

User manual

View help information to learn how to use the device and apps or configure important settings.

On the Settings screen, tap **User manual**.

About phone

Access your device's information.

On the Settings screen, tap **About phone**.

To change your device's name, tap **Edit**.

- **Status**: View various device information, such as the SIM card status, Wi-Fi MAC address, and serial number.
- **Legal information**: View legal information related to the device, such as safety information and the open source licence.
- **Software information**: View the device's software information, such as its operating system version and firmware version.
- **Battery information**: View the device's battery status and information.

Appendix

Accessibility

About Accessibility

Improve accessibility with features that make the device easier to use for users who have impaired vision, hearing, and reduced dexterity.

Launch the **Settings** app and tap **Accessibility**. You can check the accessibility feature you are using at the top of the screen. Tap ⌄ to view features you are currently using or tap **Turn off** to disable the features quickly.

Voice Assistant (Voice feedback)

Activating or deactivating Voice Assistant

When you activate Voice Assistant, the device will start voice feedback. When you tap the selected feature once, the device will read the text on the screen aloud. Tapping the feature twice will activate the feature.

Launch the **Settings** app, tap **Accessibility** → **Screen reader**, and then tap the **Voice Assistant** switch to activate it.

To deactivate Voice Assistant, tap the switch and tap anywhere on the screen twice quickly.

To view how to use Voice Assistant, tap **Tutorial**.

Some features are not available while you are using Voice Assistant.

Appendix

Controlling the screen with finger gestures

You can use various finger gestures to control the screen while you are using Voice Assistant.

One finger gestures

- Tapping: Read aloud the item under your finger. To explore the screen, place a finger on the screen and move it on the screen.
- Tapping twice: Open the selected item. While selected items are read aloud, when you hear the item you want, release your finger from the item. Then, tap anywhere on the screen twice quickly.
- Double-tapping and holding the screen: Move an item or access an available option.
- Swiping to the left: Read the previous item.
- Swiping to the right: Read the next item.
- Swiping upwards or downwards: Change the most recent contextual menu settings.
- Swiping to the left then right in one motion: Scroll up the screen.
- Swiping to the right then left in one motion: Scroll down the screen.
- Swiping upwards then downwards in one motion: Move to the first item on the screen.
- Swiping downwards then upwards in one motion: Move to the last item on the screen.

Two finger gestures

- Tapping twice: Start, pause, or resume the current action.
- Tapping three times: Check the current time, remaining battery power, and more. To change items that are read aloud, launch the **Settings** app and tap **Accessibility** → **Screen reader** → **Settings** → **Status bar information**.
- Tapping four times: Activate or deactivate voice feedback.
- Swiping to the left: Move to the next page.
- Swiping to the right: Return to the previous page.
- Swiping upwards: Scroll down the list.
- Swiping downwards: Scroll up the list.

Appendix

- Swipe upwards or downwards on the Home screen: Open the Apps screen.
- Swipe upwards or downwards on the Apps screen: Return to the Home screen.
- Swiping in any direction on the locked screen: Unlock the screen.
- Swiping downwards from the top of the screen: Open the notification panel.

Three finger gestures

- Tapping: Start reading items aloud from the top.
- Tapping twice: Start reading from the next item.
- Tapping three times: Read the last selected text and copy it to the clipboard.
- Swiping to the left or right: Open the contextual menu and scroll through the options.
- Swiping upwards or downwards: Change the text reading and selecting granularity.
- Swiping upwards then downwards in one motion: Return to the previous screen.
- Swiping downwards then upwards in one motion: Return to the Home screen.

Four finger gestures

- Tapping: Return to the previous screen.
- Tapping twice: Return to the Home screen.
- Tapping three times: Open the list of recent apps.

Using the contextual menu

While you are using Voice Assistant, swipe to the left or right with three fingers. The contextual menu will appear and the device will read the options aloud. Swipe to the left or right with three fingers to scroll through the options. When you hear the option you want, swipe upwards or downwards to use the option or adjust the settings for the option. For example, when you hear **Speech rate**, you can adjust the speech rate by swiping upwards or downwards.

Appendix

Adding and managing image labels

You can assign labels to images on the screen. The device reads aloud the labels when the images are selected. Add labels to unlabelled images by tapping the screen twice with three fingers and holding.

To manage the labels, launch the **Settings** app and tap **Accessibility** → **Screen reader** → **Settings** → **Manage custom labels**.

Configuring settings for Voice Assistant

Configure settings for Voice Assistant for your convenience.

Launch the **Settings** app and tap **Accessibility** → **Screen reader** → **Settings**.

- **Text-to-speech**: Change the settings for text-to-speech features used when Voice Assistant is activated, such as languages, speed, and more.
- **Verbosity**: Customise the detailed settings for voice feedback.
- **Mute with proximity sensor**: Set the device to pause voice feedback when you place your hand over the sensor at the top of the device.
- **Shake for continuous reading**: Set the device to read aloud the text displayed on the screen when you shake the device. You can select from various shaking intensity.
- **Speak passwords**: Set the device to read the characters aloud when you enter your password.
- **Read out caller ID**: Set the device to read the caller's name aloud when you have an incoming call.
- **Vibration feedback**: Set the device to vibrate when you control the screen, such as selecting an item.
- **Sound feedback**: Set the device to emit a sound when you control the screen, such as selecting an item. You can also adjust the volume of the sound played when you touch the screen to control it.
- **Focus on speech audio**: Set the device to turn the media volume down when the device reads an item aloud.

Appendix

- **Focus indicator**: Set the device to thicken the border of the focus indicator that appears when you tap items. You can also change the colour of the indicator.
- **Single-tap activation**: Set the device to activate the selected item with a single tap.
- **Single-tap navigation bar**: Set the device to use the buttons on the navigation bar with a single tap.
- **Quick menu**: Select contextual menu options to display when you swipe to the left or right with three fingers.
- **Manage custom labels**: Manage the labels you added.
- **Keyboard shortcuts**: Set key shortcuts to use when using an external keyboard.
- **Status bar information**: Select items to read aloud when you tap the screen three times with two fingers.
- **Developer options**: Set options for app development.

Entering text using the keyboard

To display the keyboard, tap the text input field, and then tap anywhere on the screen twice quickly.

To activate the rapid key input feature, launch the **Settings** app, tap **Accessibility** → **Screen reader**, and then tap the **Quick typing** switch to activate it.

When you touch the keyboard with your finger, the device reads aloud the character keys under your finger. When you hear the character you want, release your finger from the screen to select it. The character is entered and the device reads the text aloud.

If **Quick typing** is not activated, release your finger from the character you want, and then tap anywhere on the screen twice quickly.

This feature will appear only when Voice Assistant has been activated.

Entering additional characters

Tap and hold a key on the keyboard to enter additional characters available for the key. A pop-up window appears above the key showing available characters. To select a character, drag your finger on the pop-up window until you hear the character you want, and release it.

Appendix

Visibility enhancements

Using the high contrast theme

Apply a clear theme that displays light-coloured content on a dark background.

Launch the **Settings** app, tap **Accessibility** → **Visibility enhancements** → **High contrast theme**, and then select a theme you want.

Using the high contrast font

Adjust the colour and outline of fonts to increase the contrast between the text and the background.

Launch the **Settings** app, tap **Accessibility** → **Visibility enhancements**, and then tap the **High contrast fonts** switch to activate it.

Using the high contrast keyboard

Change the colours of the Samsung keyboard to increase the contrast between the text and the background.

Launch the **Settings** app, tap **Accessibility** → **Visibility enhancements**, and then tap the **High contrast keyboard** switch to activate it.

Displaying button shapes

Display button shapes with frames to make them stand out.

Launch the **Settings** app, tap **Accessibility** → **Visibility enhancements**, and then tap the **Show button shapes** switch to activate it.

Reversing the display colours

Improve screen visibility to help users recognise text on the screen more easily.

Launch the **Settings** app, tap **Accessibility** → **Visibility enhancements**, and then tap the **Negative colours** switch to activate it.

Appendix

Colour adjustment

Adjust how colours are displayed on the screen if you have difficulty in distinguishing colours. The device changes the colours into more recognisable colours.

Launch the **Settings** app, tap **Accessibility** → **Visibility enhancements** → **Colour adjustment**, and then tap the switch to activate it. Select an option.

To adjust the intensity of colour, drag the adjustment bar under **Intensity**.

If you select **Personalised colour**, you can personalise the colour of the screen. Follow the on-screen instructions to complete the colour adjustment procedure.

Colour lens

Adjust the screen colours if you have difficulty in reading the text.

Launch the **Settings** app, tap **Accessibility** → **Visibility enhancements** → **Colour lens**, and then tap the switch to activate it. Select a colour you want.

To adjust the transparency level, drag the adjustment bar under **Opacity**.

Reducing screen motion effects

Reduce animation effects if you are sensitive to animations or screen movement.

Launch the **Settings** app, tap **Accessibility** → **Visibility enhancements**, and then tap the **Remove animations** switch to activate it.

Using a magnifier

Activate a magnifier to zoom in on the screen to view a larger version of the content.

Launch the **Settings** app, tap **Accessibility** → **Visibility enhancements**, and then tap the **Magnifier window** switch to activate it. The magnifier will appear on the screen.

Drag the edge of the magnifier frame to move the magnifier to where you want to zoom in on the screen.

Appendix

Magnifying the screen

Magnify the screen and zoom in on a specific area.

Launch the **Settings** app and tap **Accessibility** → **Visibility enhancements** → **Magnification**.

- **Triple tap screen to magnify**: Zoom in by tapping the screen three times. To return to the normal view, tap the screen three times again.
- **Tap button to magnify**: Zoom in by tapping on the navigation bar, and then tapping where you want to magnify the screen. To return to the normal view, tap .

To explore the screen, drag two or more fingers across the magnified screen.

To adjust zoom ratio, pinch two or more fingers on the magnified screen or spread them apart.

You can also temporarily magnify the screen by tapping the screen three times and holding. Or, tap , and then tap and hold the screen. While holding the screen, drag your finger to explore the screen. Release your finger to return to the normal view.

- Keyboards and the navigation bar on the screen cannot be magnified.
- When this feature is activated, the performance of some apps may be affected.

Enlarging mouse or touchpad pointers

Enlarge the pointer when using an external mouse or touchpad.

Launch the **Settings** app, tap **Accessibility** → **Visibility enhancements**, and then tap the **Large mouse/touchpad pointer** switch to activate it.

Changing font

Change the font size and style.

Launch the **Settings** app and tap **Accessibility** → **Visibility enhancements** → **Font size and style**.

Changing screen zoom

Change the screen zoom setting.

Launch the **Settings** app and tap **Accessibility** → **Visibility enhancements** → **Screen zoom**.

Appendix

Hearing enhancements

Sound detectors

Set the device to vibrate when it detects your doorbell or a baby crying.

> While this feature is enabled, the voice recognition will not operate.

Baby crying detector

Launch the **Settings** and tap **Accessibility** → **Hearing enhancements** → **Sound detectors** → **Baby crying detector** → **Start**. The device will vibrate when it detects sound and the alert will be saved as a log.

Doorbell detector

1. Launch the **Settings** and tap **Accessibility** → **Hearing enhancements** → **Sound detectors** → **Doorbell detector**.

2. Tap **Record** to make a recording of your doorbell.

   The device will detect and record the doorbell.

3. Tap **Test** and ring your doorbell to check if it is recorded correctly. When the device detects the doorbell sound, tap **Start**.

   To change the doorbell sound, tap **Change doorbell sound**.

   The device will vibrate when it detects sound and the alert will be saved as a log.

Turning off all sounds

Set the device to mute all device sounds, such as media sounds, and the caller's voice during a call.

Launch the **Settings** app, tap **Accessibility** → **Hearing enhancements**, and then tap the **Mute all sounds** switch to activate it.

Appendix

Adjusting the sound balance

Set the device to adjust the sound balance when using an earphone.

1 Connect an earphone to the device and wear it.

2 Launch the **Settings** app and tap **Accessibility** → **Hearing enhancements**.

3 Drag the adjustment bar under **Left/right sound balance** to the left or right and adjust the sound balance.

Mono audio

Mono output combines stereo sound into one signal that is played through all earphone speakers. Use this if you have a hearing impairment or if a single earbud is more convenient.

Launch the **Settings** app, tap **Accessibility** → **Hearing enhancements**, and then tap the **Mono audio** switch to activate it.

Caption settings

Launch the **Settings** app, tap **Accessibility** → **Hearing enhancements** → **Samsung subtitles (CC)** or **Google subtitles (CC)**, and then tap the switch to activate it.

Select an option for configuring the caption settings.

Speech-to-text

The device records your voice and simultaneously converts it to on-screen text.

1 Launch the **Settings** app and tap **Accessibility** → **Hearing enhancements** → **Speech-to-text**.

2 Tap and record with the microphone.

3 When you are finished recording, tap **DONE**.

 To view recorded files or change the voice memo system language, launch the **Voice Recorder** app.

Appendix

Interaction and dexterity

Universal switch

You can control the touchscreen by connecting an external switch, by tapping the screen, or by using head movements and face gestures.

1 Launch the **Settings** app and tap **Accessibility** → **Interaction and dexterity** → **Universal switch**.

2 Read the on-screen instructions and tap **Done**.

3 Tap the switch to activate it.

4 If the universal switches are not registered on the device, tap **Add switch** and set switches to control the device.

> To activate the universal switch feature, at least one switch must be registered on the device.

To set switches to control the device, tap the switch under **Switches**.

To deactivate this feature, press the Power key and the Volume Up key simultaneously.

Assistant menu

Displaying the assistive shortcut icon

Set the device to display the assistive shortcut icon for accessing apps, features, and settings. You can easily control the device by tapping the assistive menus in the icon.

1 Launch the **Settings** app and tap **Accessibility** → **Interaction and dexterity** → **Assistant menu**.

2 Tap the switch to activate it.

The assistive shortcut icon appears at the bottom right of the screen.

To adjust the assistant shortcut icon's transparency level, drag the adjustment bar under **Transparency**.

Appendix

Accessing assistive menus

The assistive shortcut icon appears as a floating icon for easy access to the assistive menus from any screen.

When you tap the assistive shortcut icon, the icon expands slightly and the assistive menus appear on the icon. Tap the left or right arrow to move to other panels or swipe to the left or right to select other menus.

Using the cursor

On the assistive menu, tap **Cursor**. You can control the screen using small finger movements on the touch area. Drag your finger on the touch area to move the cursor. Also, tap the screen to select items under the cursor.

Use the following options:

- ≪ / ≫ : Scroll left or right on the screen.
- ≪ / ≫ : Scroll up or down the screen.
- ⊕ : Magnify the area where the cursor is located.

Turn off the Always On Display before using this feature.

- ✲ : Change the touchpad and cursor settings.
- ✥ : Move the touch area to another location.
- ✕ : Close the touch area.

Using enhanced assistive menus

Set the device to display enhanced assistive menus for selected apps.

Launch the **Settings** app, tap **Accessibility** → **Interaction and dexterity** → **Assistant menu** → **Assistant plus**, tap the switch to activate it, and then select apps.

Click after pointer stops

Set the device to select an item automatically when you place the mouse pointer over the item.

Launch the **Settings** app, tap **Accessibility** → **Interaction and dexterity**, and then tap the **Click after pointer stops** switch to activate it.

Appendix

Answering or ending calls

Change the method for answering or ending calls.

Launch the **Settings** app and tap **Accessibility** → **Interaction and dexterity** → **Answering and ending calls**.

Select the desired method.

Using single tap mode

When an alarm sounds or a call comes in, tap the button to stop the alarm, or answer or reject the call instead of dragging the button.

Launch the **Settings** app and tap **Accessibility** → **Interaction and dexterity**, and then tap the **Single tap to swipe** switch to activate it.

Easy screen turn on

Turn on the screen by moving your hand above the sensor at the top of the device. You can turn on the screen without pressing a key. When you use this feature, place the device on a flat surface with the screen facing upwards or hold the device securely to prevent it from moving.

Launch the **Settings** app, tap **Accessibility** → **Interaction and dexterity**, and then tap the **Easy screen turn on** switch to activate it.

Interaction control

Activate interaction control mode to restrict the device's reaction to inputs while using apps.

1 Launch the **Settings** app and tap **Accessibility** → **Interaction and dexterity** → **Interaction control**.

2 Tap the switch to activate it.

3 Press and hold the Power key and the Volume Up key simultaneously while using an app.

Appendix

4 Adjust the size of the frame or draw a line around an area that you want to restrict.

5 Tap **Done**.

The device displays the restricted area. The restricted area will not react when you touch it and the device's keys will be disabled. However, you can enable functions for the Power key, Volume key, and keyboard in interaction control mode.

To deactivate interaction control mode, press and hold the Power key and the Volume Up key simultaneously.

To set the device to lock the screen after deactivating interaction control mode, launch the **Settings** screen, tap **Accessibility** → **Interaction and dexterity** → **Interaction control**, and then tap the **Lock when deactivated** switch to activate it.

Touch and hold delay

Set the recognition time for tapping and holding the screen.

Launch the **Settings** app, tap **Accessibility** → **Interaction and dexterity** → **Touch and hold delay**, and then select an option.

Tap duration

Set the duration you must touch the screen for the device to recognise it as a tap.

Launch the **Settings** app, tap **Accessibility** → **Interaction and dexterity** → **Tap duration**, tap the switch to activate it, and then set the time.

Ignore repeated touches

Set the device to recognise only the first tap within a set time when you tap the screen repeatedly.

Launch the **Settings** app, tap **Accessibility** → **Interaction and dexterity** → **Ignore repeated touches**, tap the switch to activate it, and then set the time.

Appendix

Advanced settings

Launching accessibility features quickly

Set to open accessibility features quickly.

Launch the **Settings** app, tap **Accessibility** → **Advanced settings** → **Power and Volume up keys**, and then tap the switch to activate it. Then, select an accessibility feature to open when you simultaneously press the Power key and the Volume Up key.

You can access the following accessibility features:

- Accessibility
- Voice Assistant
- Universal switch
- Magnifier window
- Negative colours
- Colour adjustment
- Colour lens
- Interaction control
- High contrast fonts

Launching the shortcut services quickly

Set to start a shortcut services quickly.

Launch the **Settings** app, tap **Accessibility** → **Advanced settings** → **Volume up and down keys**, and then tap the switch to activate it. Then, tap **Selected service** and select a shortcut service to start when you simultaneously press and hold the Volume Up key and the Volume Down key for three seconds.

You can access the following shortcut services:

- Universal switch
- Voice Assistant

Appendix

Setting light notification

Set the device to blink the flash or the screen when an alarm sounds or when you have notifications, such as incoming calls or new messages.

Launch the **Settings** app, tap **Accessibility** → **Advanced settings** → **Flash notification**, and then tap the switches next to the options you want to activate.

Notification reminders

Set the device to alert you to notifications that you have not checked at the interval.

Launch the **Settings** app, tap **Accessibility** → **Advanced settings** → **Notification reminders**, and then tap the switch to activate it.

To set the device to vibrate and play a notification sound when you have unchecked notifications, tap the **Vibrate when sound plays** switch to activate it.

To set an interval between alerts, tap **Remind every**.

To set apps to alert you to notifications, tap the switches next to apps under **Selected reminders** to activate it.

Adding voice recordings to voice labels

You can use voice labels to distinguish objects of similar shape by attaching labels to them. You can record and assign a voice recording to an NFC-enabled voice label. The voice recording is played back when you place your device near the label.

> Turn on the NFC feature before using this feature.

1 Launch the **Settings** app and tap **Accessibility** → **Advanced settings** → **Voice Label**.
   The voice recorder will launch.

2 Tap ● to start recording. Speak into the microphone.

3 When you are finished recording, tap **DONE** to stop.

4 Hold the back of your device over the voice label.
   The information in the voice recording will be written to the voice label.

Appendix

Direction lock

Create a directional combination to unlock the screen.

1 Launch the **Settings** app, tap **Accessibility** → **Advanced settings** → **Direction lock**, and then tap the switch to activate it.

2 Drag your finger up, down, left, or right six to eight times, and then tap **CONTINUE**.

3 Draw the direction combination again to verify it and tap **CONFIRM**.

Installed services

View accessibility services installed on the device.

Launch the **Settings** app and tap **Accessibility** → **Installed services**.

Appendix

Troubleshooting

Before contacting a Samsung Service Centre, please attempt the following solutions. Some situations may not apply to your device.

When you turn on your device or while you are using the device, it prompts you to enter one of the following codes:

- Password: When the device lock feature is enabled, you must enter the password you set for the device.
- PIN: When using the device for the first time or when the PIN requirement is enabled, you must enter the PIN supplied with the SIM or USIM card. You can disable this feature by using the Lock SIM card menu.
- PUK: Your SIM or USIM card is blocked, usually as a result of entering your PIN incorrectly several times. You must enter the PUK supplied by your service provider.
- PIN2: When you access a menu requiring the PIN2, you must enter the PIN2 supplied with the SIM or USIM card. For more information, contact your service provider.

Your device displays network or service error messages

- When you are in areas with weak signals or poor reception, you may lose reception. Move to another area and try again. While moving, error messages may appear repeatedly.
- You cannot access some options without a subscription. For more information, contact your service provider.

Your device does not turn on

When the battery is completely discharged, your device will not turn on. Fully charge the battery before turning on the device.

Appendix

The touchscreen responds slowly or improperly

- If you attach a screen protector or optional accessories to the touchscreen, the touchscreen may not function properly.
- If you are wearing gloves, if your hands are not clean while touching the touchscreen, or if you tap the screen with sharp objects or your fingertips, the touchscreen may malfunction.
- The touchscreen may malfunction in humid conditions or when exposed to water.
- Restart your device to clear any temporary software bugs.
- Ensure that your device software is updated to the latest version.
- If the touchscreen is scratched or damaged, visit a Samsung Service Centre.

Your device freezes or encounters a fatal error

Try the following solutions. If the problem is still not resolved, contact a Samsung Service Centre.

Restarting the device

If your device freezes or hangs, you may need to close apps or turn off the device and turn it on again.

Forcing restart

If your device is frozen and unresponsive, press and hold the Power key and the Volume Down key simultaneously for more than 7 seconds to restart it.

Resetting the device

If the methods above do not solve your problem, perform a factory data reset.

Launch the **Settings** app and tap **General management** → **Reset** → **Factory data reset** → **Reset** → **Delete all**. Before performing the factory data reset, remember to make backup copies of all important data stored in the device.

Appendix

Calls are not connected

- Ensure that you have accessed the right cellular network.
- Ensure that you have not set call barring for the phone number you are dialling.
- Ensure that you have not set call barring for the incoming phone number.

Others cannot hear you speaking on a call

- Ensure that you are not covering the built-in microphone.
- Ensure that the microphone is close to your mouth.
- If using an earphone, ensure that it is properly connected.

Sound echoes during a call

Adjust the volume by pressing the Volume key or move to another area.

A cellular network or the Internet is often disconnected or audio quality is poor

- Ensure that you are not blocking the device's internal antenna.
- When you are in areas with weak signals or poor reception, you may lose reception. You may have connectivity problems due to issues with the service provider's base station. Move to another area and try again.
- When using the device while moving, wireless network services may be disabled due to issues with the service provider's network.

The battery icon is empty

Your battery is low. Charge the battery.

Appendix

The battery does not charge properly (For Samsung-approved chargers)

- Ensure that the charger is connected properly.
- Visit a Samsung Service Centre and have the battery replaced.

The battery depletes faster than when first purchased

- When you expose the device or the battery to very cold or very hot temperatures, the useful charge may be reduced.
- Battery consumption will increase when you use certain features or apps, such as GPS, games, or the Internet.
- The battery is consumable and the useful charge will get shorter over time.

Error messages appear when launching the camera

Your device must have sufficient available memory and battery power to operate the camera app. If you receive error messages when launching the camera, try the following:

- Charge the battery.
- Free some memory by transferring files to a computer or deleting files from your device.
- Restart the device. If you are still having trouble with the camera app after trying these tips, contact a Samsung Service Centre.

Photo quality is poorer than the preview

- The quality of your photos may vary, depending on the surroundings and the photography techniques you use.
- If you take photos in dark areas, at night, or indoors, image noise may occur or images may be out of focus.

Appendix

Error messages appear when opening multimedia files

If you receive error messages or multimedia files do not play when you open them on your device, try the following:

- Free some memory by transferring files to a computer or deleting files from your device.
- Ensure that the music file is not Digital Rights Management (DRM)-protected. If the file is DRM-protected, ensure that you have the appropriate licence or key to play the file.
- Ensure that the file formats are supported by the device. If a file format is not supported, such as DivX or AC3, install an app that supports it. To confirm the file formats that your device supports, visit www.samsung.com.
- Your device supports photos and videos captured with the device. Photos and videos captured by other devices may not work properly.
- Your device supports multimedia files that are authorised by your network service provider or providers of additional services. Some content circulated on the Internet, such as ringtones, videos, or wallpapers, may not work properly.

Bluetooth is not working well

If another Bluetooth device is not located or there are connection problems or performance malfunctions, try the following:

- Ensure that the device you wish to connect with is ready to be scanned or connected to.
- Ensure that your device and the other Bluetooth device are within the maximum Bluetooth range (10 m).
- On your device, launch the **Settings** app, tap **Connections**, and then tap the **Bluetooth** switch to re-activate it.
- On your device, launch the **Settings** app, tap **General management** → **Reset** → **Reset network settings** → **Reset** → **Reset** to reset network settings. You may lose registered information when performing the reset.

If the tips above do not solve the problem, contact a Samsung Service Centre.

Appendix

A connection is not established when you connect the device to a computer

- Ensure that the USB cable you are using is compatible with your device.
- Ensure that you have the proper driver installed and updated on your computer.
- If you are a Windows XP user, ensure that you have Windows XP Service Pack 3 or higher installed on your computer.

Your device cannot find your current location

GPS signals may be obstructed in some locations, such as indoors. Set the device to use Wi-Fi or a mobile network to find your current location in these situations.

Data stored in the device has been lost

Always make backup copies of all important data stored in the device. Otherwise, you cannot restore data if it is corrupted or lost. Samsung is not responsible for the loss of data stored in the device.

A small gap appears around the outside of the device case

- This gap is a necessary manufacturing feature and some minor rocking or vibration of parts may occur.
- Over time, friction between parts may cause this gap to expand slightly.

There is not enough space in the device's storage

Delete unnecessary data, such as cache, using the device care feature or manually delete unused apps or files to free up storage space.

Appendix

The Apps button does not appear on the Home screen

Without using the Apps button, you can open the Apps screen by swiping upwards or downwards on the Home screen. To display the Apps button at the bottom of the Home screen, launch the **Settings** app, tap **Display** → **Home screen**, and then tap the **Apps button** switch to activate it.

The Home button does not appear

The navigation bar containing the Home button may disappear while using certain apps or features. To view the navigation bar, drag upwards from the bottom of the screen.

Bixby does not respond

- Restart your device to clear any temporary software bugs.
- Ensure that your device software is updated to the latest version.
- If you are still having trouble with Bixby after trying these tips, contact a Samsung Service Centre.

The screen brightness adjustment bar does not appear on the notification panel

Open the notification panel by dragging the status bar downwards, and then drag the notification panel downwards. Tap ∨ next to the brightness adjustment bar and tap the **Show control on top** switch to activate it.

Samsung Cloud does not work

- Ensure that you are connected to a network properly.
- During a Samsung Cloud's service check, you cannot use Samsung Cloud. Try again later.

Appendix

The device does not recognise my irises from the locked screen

- Ensure that nothing obstructing the iris recognition camera and LED and try again.
- If light conditions are very different from when you registered your irises, the device may not recognise your irises. Move to another location and try again.
- Ensure that the device is not moving or tilted too much.

Removing the battery

- **To remove the battery, contact an authorised service centre. To obtain battery removal instructions, please visit** www.samsung.com/global/ecodesign_energy.
- For your safety, you **must not attempt to remove** the battery. If the battery is not properly removed, it may lead to damage to the battery and device, cause personal injury, and/or result in the device being unsafe.
- Samsung does not accept liability for any damage or loss (whether in contract or tort, including negligence) which may arise from failure to precisely follow these warnings and instructions, other than death or personal injury caused by Samsung's negligence.

Copyright

Copyright © 2018 Samsung Electronics

This manual is protected under international copyright laws.

No part of this manual may be reproduced, distributed, translated, or transmitted in any form or by any means, electronic or mechanical, including photocopying, recording, or storing in any information storage and retrieval system, without the prior written permission of Samsung Electronics.

Trademarks

- SAMSUNG and the SAMSUNG logo are registered trademarks of Samsung Electronics.
- Bluetooth® is a registered trademark of Bluetooth SIG, Inc. worldwide.
- Wi-Fi®, Wi-Fi Protected Setup™, Wi-Fi Direct™, Wi-Fi CERTIFIED™, and the Wi-Fi logo are registered trademarks of the Wi-Fi Alliance.
- Manufactured under license from Dolby Laboratories. Dolby, Dolby Atmos, and the double-D symbol are trademarks of Dolby Laboratories.
- All other trademarks and copyrights are the property of their respective owners.

HEVC Advance™
Covered by Patents at patentlist.hevcadvance.com

Made in the
USA
Columbia, SC

78325829R10147